Think. Drink. EAT. MOVE.

4 Steps to YES

Jeanne M. Stafford

BOMBARDIER BOOKS

Thanksgiving, 2018

My dear Sharon,

Happy reading to one of my first messengers of YES and my dear pal.

To James and Harry, my princes

Love and see you many more times to celebrate

Jeanne

TABLE OF CONTENTS

FOREWORD

by Susan Lucci

I have known Jeanne Stafford since she was a child. I watched her grow up and have a career in politics and enjoyed the chance to support her work when she served in the Giuliani administration.

I was there when she walked down the aisle on the day of her wedding and I have watched her manage many events in her life since then.

When Jeanne transformed yet again into a professional speaker it was my joy to join her as the guest speaker for her intimate Networking Dinner in New York City. It was there I had the chance to meet the incredible audience she serves in the work she does now cheering all of us to embrace YES.

At the time Jeanne and I met to discuss her book and her Networking event, I shared the first time I was moved by the word YES. I heard this song—and her album *Liza With a Z*—for the first time when I was in college. The song and the fact that Liza Minelli sang it made a lasting impact on me.

Every word in Liza Minelli's song describes what Jeanne is speaking and writing about. The lyrics start with a promise, "When opportunity comes your way...." Then move to a challenge: "You'll never win if you never play...." And conclude with the solution: "Say YES...."

These words speak to so many of us who need to do something and realize the next step starts with us saying we can and we will when we say YES!

There could not be a better time to communicate the steps to greater positivity. There couldn't be a better time for those of us in the public eye to share how we take risks and try new things all the time.

As an actress and author, I can tell you it takes a lot to share parts of yourself for all the world to see and read and keep. It needs to be done with thoughtfulness and in simple steps so others can understand how your practice of improvement can become theirs.

Jeanne Stafford is sunshine—and in *Think. Drink. Eat. Move. 4 Steps to YES*, she shines her light of positivity on how YOU can reach your own goals.

How can you accomplish long-term looking and feeling your best? Jeanne keeps it simple and fun with your beautifully illustrated 4-step Workbook! She shares her personal challenges and recipe for success—imbued with her signature "YES" mantra and can-do attitude! She breaks it down and gives you the go-to tools to move you to where you dream of being.

I love Jeanne Stafford—and her book!

INTRODUCTION

WHO AM I?

I am a mother of two teenaged boys, a professional speaker, a comedy improviser, the oldest of five children, Irish Catholic, a girly girl, spiritually adventurous, a fierce friend, a proud Republican, and a great American. I was once married, and now I am not. I have been on most dating sites you read about (and that may be another book). At this moment and most moments, I'm happy more often than I am not.

As a professional speaker, I train people to *Say YES to Every Space They Enter* and to think like an improviser so they can communicate without a script. I am writing a book about communication techniques I uncovered while on the special education track with my son. This is not that book; this book needed to happen *first*.

WHY ***THIS*** BOOK?

Over the past few years as I interacted with people from the stage and in one-on-one conversations, the topic would always get to my energy, health, and weight. I'd empathize with their challenges in the weight department and offer suggestions to increase their energy levels. I shared that I had lost forty pounds over many years. In the time leading up to my fiftieth birthday, I had promised myself I would be the weight I was when I was twenty-five years old. I had fifteen pounds to go as of my forty-ninth birthday and *I did it*!

They'd ask, "How did you do it?" and "What worked?" and "What did you eat?" I'd answer their questions and give them suggestions and then they'd say, "You should write about it, make a list of what you eat and tell people what kind of exercise you do."

I thought, "I'll get to that book sometime. Not now, though, because the book I am writing at this time is more important. It ties into what I am modeling my entire business around and that is more important than a book about health and weight."

Then I was with a client who asked me what I did to keep myself sane. She asked what I ate and what my favorite exercise was. Then it happened again after I gave a keynote. Someone came up to me and asked if I ever had trouble sleeping and asked if I meditated on a regular basis.

At that moment, it came to me: I can write something shorter! Telling people about my journey with weight, food energy, and happiness can come out of me in record time because sharing tips is a natural part of me and the people I'm meeting and working with would like to know how I do what I do.

Why should I be the messenger of this message?

Any one of us can be a powerful messenger for the real-life experiences we have. While I am not a doctor or a nutritionist, I *am* a woman whose body has been through pregnancy, childbirth, surgery, and substantial weight fluctuations. When I tell my story and share my results, someone may be helped.

Better yet, someone may be inspired to write *their* story and *that* would thrill me!

Like many of you, I have read it all and read it all again, and I have tried it all and tried it all again. From as far back as when I was a teenager, I have sought to lose weight. I've done the Grapefruit Diet, the Cabbage Soup Diet, Weight Watchers, Jenny Craig, various cleanses, Atkins, SlimFast, and Lean Cuisine. To be honest, I went on a drug—that was eventually recalled—that suppressed my appetite, or I should say eliminated it. With *every* one of these methods mentioned, I lost weight. And I gained it back when I stopped.

In my fifty years on this planet, I have lost and gained *a lot* of weight *a lot* of times.

In the past, when I thought about my weight, I thought about what I still needed to do. I thought about how everything would be better when I could fit into that dress or those pants or be seen in a bathing suit without being wrapped in my favorite cover-up. The weight thing felt as if it were standing in front of me and blocking me.

It was time to create a routine to stay healthy with everything that went into my body and *every* move I made. This happened over time. As I learned the patience and faith necessary to enjoy myself, eating became effortless, my energy level improved and happiness ensued.

I like to learn from people who achieve their goals, don't you? It's pleasing to hear how someone becomes successful. It's comforting when they share that it wasn't easy. I see myself in the possibility of their new state. That is why I am allowing myself to be a messenger of health, happiness and feeling great at fifty years young.

What will I talk about?

"How can we bottle your energy, Jeanne?"

This is a question I have been asked quite a few times. People want to know how I achieve and maintain my optimism and high energy level when I'm speaking to a large group or in personal conversations.

The answer is, *you* can do this too! You *have* this energy source yourself. The fact is, I am not happy *every* minute of every day, but I *am* able to get in the zone and back-to-happy *fast*.

In the pages of this book, I'll share the stories that led me to strategies that helped me get back on track throughout my action-packed days. These strategies are rooted in the way I think as a performer of comedy improv. Shortly after I started studying improv, I began to see how *every* space I entered offered me an opportunity to move forward.

When things seem out of control, I can remember the routine I have created with my thoughts, food, and movement and have a place to check in. I know I'll feel better because I've created a personal frame of reference to return to my center—My YES—and feel successful again.

When you establish this routine with yourself, you uncover the fearless person inside of you who's ready to take risks and generate something new.

These aren't rituals that go away once your "goal" is reached. *This* is the ritual *you* create for *yourself* that is tailor-made by *you*. This ritual is the gift you give to yourself.

This is not a diet. This is a lifetime practice for your mind *and* body. This is a new way of thinking.

My prayer is that this book helps you to feel the way *you* want to feel so you can get where *you* want to go. It's infused with steps to uncover confidence and momentum created by *you*, nothing else and *no one* else but *you*!

You will feel in charge and you will have power. Most importantly, you will learn to trust yourself. You will learn what makes you tick and how to listen to your body. You will learn a little bit about improv comedy and how thinking like an improviser helps you get back into the space you need to be.

I started studying Improv Comedy in New York City in 1998. After taking my first class, I never stopped studying, and I never stopped performing. I consider myself a student of improv and I will always be a student. There is *that* much to learn.

Improv is the lens through which I communicate to myself and to others. By studying improv, I release the performer in me. When I'm connected to the YES in every space I enter, I'm more fully present. My energy is operating as it is meant to be.

What is improv?

Improv is a form of theater performed without a script with very few, if any, props and which includes audience participation. Improvisers are trained to be present in the scene so they may see and hear the offers of the other actors or hear offers in the silence in the scene. An "offer" is anything said or any action taken with one actor to the other in the scene. Offers are to be accepted and examples of this are below. When this is done well, something funny happens and the audience laughs.

There are many things that keep a scene from going where it is supposed to go. Control is one of them. If an actor is looking to control what happens, they will be saying NO to offers and will keep transformations from happening.

When actors say (and think) YES, they are allowing their character to be affected and transformed by relationships and events happening in the scene.

When you really dive into the nuts and bolts of this practice, you begin to see where you are acting out some of the things that keep you stuck in real life.

For example, as an improviser, I often tried to fix scenes in which it looked like something bad was going to happen. If someone broke a leg, I tried to fix it; if someone died, I tried to bring them back to life. I was trying to "fix" events in improv the way I was trying to "fix" things in life.

For a long time, I made my directors crazy because I was completely unconscious of what I was doing. When I started to pay attention to this, I made the connection to my personal life.

The act of playing fixer in every space I entered was draining and kept me from seeing and feeling what was right in front of me.

As I was blocked in scenes, I was blocked in life.

Once I realized this, I created a balance of letting things happen more than I sought to control outcomes. The formula I've created helps me to feel energetic and happy and embraces the principle of saying YES.

Saying *YES to Every Space You Enter* means being ready to learn something new and being content with what is. With this thinking, I have created a reservoir of energy for myself. The more I do it, the more expanded the reservoir becomes.

How improv works

Actors act out scenes in an improv show based on offers from the audience. Before the scene begins, the actors ask the audience for suggestions, such as *who* they are (the audience might suggest something like a baker or an electrician) and *where* they are (the audience might suggest something like a park or a space ship). The actors accept those offers from the audience and become the characters they have been given in the spaces they have been given and the scene begins!

There are many different kinds of improv shows and different levels of audience participation. For the sake of this quick lesson, here are the overarching themes.

A comedy improviser walks onto a stage to create a scene with one or more improvisers and carries an awareness of a few simple principles.

1. Their mind is free of thought. They are out of their head.
2. They are open to anything that happens.
3. They are ready to uncover a relationship and describe who these suggested characters are to each other and what the stakes are between them.
4. They are looking to say YES, establishing relationships, and being transformed in the scene.

Once a relationship is uncovered, they move the scene along by saying "YES, AND" to every offer presented. For example, actor number one could exclaim, "I found a love letter in your pocket while I was doing your laundry!" and this most likely makes actor number two the lover/partner/spouse of actor number one. The scene moves forward when actor number two accepts that offer and says something like, "Yes, and I'm cheating on you."

If actor number two said, "that wasn't my letter," they would be saying NO to the offer by actor number one. By accepting this is who they are and that is what they've done, they are furthering the dialogue describing their relationship and the event unfolding. Now there is an opportunity for the audience to find out what might happen next.

The improviser's goal is to find the event or conflict and to be affected by that. The event/conflict in this example is the discovery of the letter. Now the scene becomes interesting to the audience. The stakes are raised. The improvisers are mindful to keep saying YES. They will accept every offer. Laughter may ensue.

Why is this a handbook?

I'd like my readers to record thoughts and ideas that come to them as they read. No matter what is going on in my life, I do this too. As my audience reads this book, I would like them to be able to do the same. As they write, I hope they uncover how they can feel successful and happy in *all* the spaces they enter.

My work as a professional speaker is an outlet for everything I'm curious about. I'm curious about words. I'm curious about how patterns of communication keep us where we are or move us to where we want to go. I'm curious about what makes people joyful and want to laugh out loud.

As an improv comedy performer for almost twenty years, I've enjoyed the way scenes develop with ease and deliver entertainment to audiences. Improvisers see the YES in the space.

Writing this book is a complete departure from what many think should be the next step in the trajectory of my business. Some would tell me that I may confuse my audience by writing a book about health, happiness, weight, and being fifty years young.

As I celebrated my fiftieth I wrote a piece for the *Huffington Post* called, "50 Things I'm Taking Into My Next 50 Years." My audience read it, shared it, and commented on it in a way they hadn't before. It was one of the messages screaming to me from the universe, which said, "Write this small, simple book with a big, sophisticated message. Say YES to this offer, Jeanne!"

Three of the Messengers Who Led Me to This Book

My sister, Karen

I was on the phone with my sister and she had just referred to me as a "skinny bitch." (*Please Note*: I am not skinny. Skinny is a word people use when they are proud of you for losing *any* weight. Back to my story...) I laughed and told her I didn't feel skinny. I felt better than skinny. The size I was now felt natural. I felt like I was where I was always meant to be.

She said, "Mmm...that's good. You should tell people that. You should write about that."

My college chum, Jane

During lunch with my friend Jane for her fiftieth birthday, the topic of weight came up again. She had lost and put back on weight (like all of us) and asked me what I was doing to keep mine off. I told her about some of my daily practices around food, thoughts, movement, meditation, and prayer.

In her thank-you note for the birthday lunch, she wrote, "P.S. Please send me the weight loss tricks and breathing techniques that work for you...OHMMMM."

My friend from Rwanda, Immaculée

I was having lunch with fellow speaker, Immaculée Ilibagiza, and her sister-in-law, Dative Uwamahoro. Dative was visiting from Rwanda where they both grew up. She was working on her English and seemed self-conscious about it. Because of that, she didn't make a lot of eye contact when we first sat down. I suggested I would have a glass of wine with lunch and asked if they wanted to join me. Immaculée said Dative was working hard to lose weight and didn't want to drink because of that. I told her about some of the things I did to lose fifteen pounds by my fiftieth birthday and, when Immaculée translated what I said, Dative smiled and her eyes locked on me. She said something in her language and Immaculée looked at me and said, "She wants to know *how*."

Our mindset around weight is a universal challenge.

It was time for me to pay attention to *all* these messages. It was time for me to embrace the *simple* idea to write a "how-to" for so many people looking to get to that place that feels "natural."

This is a short, fun handbook and I hope you feel you are a part of it as you read. I will share how I became aware of a new way of thinking and what I do to get back on track when life takes me off course. This is a step-by-step guide to uncover your way to feel natural, peaceful, and strong.

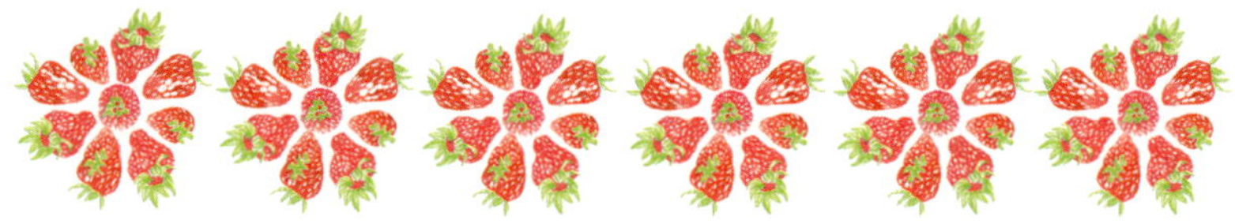

Four Sections

To make this simple and to outline a new daily thinking practice for you, I divided the routine into FOUR sections:

Think | *Drink* | *Eat* | *Move*

We all have a lot going on in our lives. By breaking this book up into parts, it's easier to digest. I also *love* the number "four" as I have a personal connection to it. I was born in the fourth month, April, plus it's an even number and I love even numbers! I also seek to make connections in all communication. The number "four" has spiritual meaning symbolizing a strong foundation and is the number of stability and order.

THE WORKBOOK SECTIONS

After you read each of the four sections, reflect on where you are now and write your notes here in the book. My goal is for this book to feel like a gift you are giving yourself and one that you will want to give to others. It's fun to look at and hold and there are *many* spaces to write down what you're thinking. There are sections for you to write at the end of each chapter and then a planner at the end of the book to chart your four-week path to YES. I'll call these sections for you to write your notes, The Space of YES for YOU!

These four steps model the fact that *you* are in control of how *you* feel. Sometimes giving yourself permission to have that much power is the only thing preventing you from being where you want to be. We all have this power. Let's seize it together!

Celebrate the routine you create.

Let's get started.

Start your day with Think.

Our minds and our thoughts are incredibly powerful, and I've watched a lot of people give their power away by forgetting this. When you get your power back, you regain control of your life. You uncover the gifts you have to give others and then you set those gifts free. The pattern continues and others learn from you how to do it too.

Gratitude

Your first thoughts are presented to you when you wake up. What you think at the very first moment you open your eyes is an opportunity to set the tone for the day.

I once asked my grandfather what the first thing was that he thought of every day. He said, "I wake up, I look at my bride and I say, 'Katie, let's get the hell outta here!'" He was telling me he was happy to wake up and happier to wake up with my grandmother and have something to do. His enthusiasm for life was contagious. It was nice to learn he started his day with that much gratitude.

I think of that when I wake up. I'm happy to be up. I'm happy to have the day and, because I'm a prayerful person, I give a shout-out to God and to the Blessed Mother.

There's your first step to health and satisfaction. Think gratitude before you even get out of bed. Be grateful for the day. Salute it and then get out of bed.

Move from the bed to the next place to think, the bathroom, and say hello to the scale. Negative thoughts weigh heavily on the heart and hips. Think of the scale to create light for yourself.

The scale

The scale is your friend, your really, *really* good friend that knows *everything*! Check in with it *every* day after you get out of bed and do your "thing." If the scale has been your enemy, you can make it your friend. It's along for the long haul, a friend that will give you the truth and stand by you—or under you—every day!

The visit to the scale is a gift you give to yourself. Over the decades, the message the scale has been giving me has shifted. That is why it's important that I kept up with it. I now have a better understanding of the scale and the scale remains my very clear, very honest friend.

The two-week rule

As I got closer to age fifty, I learned it takes at least two weeks to shed as little as two to three pounds. As a result, I'm more mindful of what I eat all the time because otherwise, I'll always feel like I'm behind all the time. This helps me to be patient and feel I have a formula to work with.

When I was in my twenties and thirties, feedback from the scale happened much faster and it was easier to gauge what clothes I would fit into in a week. For example, something I ate today would be reflected—or not—on the scale the next day. This is not the case at fifty. Nope. Planning and perseverance are the themes of the two-week rule.

Now I know that if I want to plan to feel a certain way, I need to be really vigilant more than two weeks out. To turn the discussion with myself into a positive one, I think of the exciting things ahead of me. That's the gift I'm giving myself.

The scale tells you where you are and that's all you need to know. Where you are, here and now. The decisions you make throughout the day can keep you where you are or get you to where you want to be.

The scale is the truth. What I want you to do is imagine what it would be like *not* to have somewhere to check in where you can get the truth.

The scale helps you develop a relationship with yourself. No one else is there. It's just you and the scale and the number it gives you in seconds.

Let's talk about that number. For most of us, that is an important number. It takes two weeks for a scale to accurately represent what you did or did not do. Be patient and build faith in yourself that the number is going down.

This daily practice connects you with that number the moment you get up. You learn about *your* body and its relationship with food, water, alcohol, sugar, movement, and sleep.

Also, weigh yourself at different times in the day, a few times a month. Do this so you can understand *how much* of what you eat causes the scale to fluctuate more. For example, during the summer I often retain more water and it may mess with the number I think I'm going to reach. I'm a little more patient as a result and usually will eat a lot less knowing this.

Your goal is swift engagement with the scale. Make it a partner in how you think about and what you know about your weight.

Meditation and prayer

Meditation and prayer are food for your heart and your head. You really need a healthy heart and your head always needs a break from what's in it. I feel like I'm giving myself the greatest gift when I do these two things in the morning. The ritual now feels like I'm starting my day with a vacation and I don't even need to spend a dime to get this feeling. Now I feel good about other things I once thought I didn't have control over.

Meditation

I started meditating about four years ago because I felt my thoughts were going to give me a heart attack. After a lot of chaos in my personal life, I knew I needed to do something to manage my fear and paralyzing thoughts that were keeping me from thriving.

With a friend, I visited Omega Retreat Center in Rhinebeck, New York, to hear Brian Weiss. Doctor Weiss is the author of *Many Lives, Many Masters* and numerous bestselling titles. His books and talks address past life regression therapy, which is a practice to help people learn more about themselves. His clients and audiences learn to sharpen their intuition when they are tuned into their past lives. The three days we spent learning how to strengthen our intuition was a wonderful distraction from what was happening in my life.

While eating in the cafeteria at Omega, I sat with people who were at another retreat with Tara Brach, a meditation teacher and author of *True Refuge, Finding Peace and Freedom in Your Own Awakened Heart*. They were captivated by her and said the transformations they were experiencing were profound. She made things simple, and they could not get enough. In addition to learning more about my intuition with Brian Weiss, I left determined to start a daily meditation practice. Tara Brach would be my guide.

I learned that sometimes you follow your intuition to do something specific in your life as I did with my curiosity around past life regression. I arrived with an open mind and heart and ending up learning about Tara Brach. This is an example about how taking care of how I think helps me to invite something new and helpful into my life.

I went home and started downloading Tara Brach's free meditations. My favorite—and the one I stuck with for most of the first year—was "Taking Refuge in the Beloved." It talks about the ego and our power over it. Each time I listen to the same recording, I hear something new. This told me how much the ego keeps us in our heads and that it was time for me to figure out *how* to get out of mine. Ironically, "getting out of your head" is the most important practice of every improviser in a scene.

The Meditation Sources I Recommend Most Often

Tara Brach

Tarabrach.com is my favorite. Tara offers free meditations and recordings of her events. Her voice is soothing. Her calming style will keep you focused. Tara also offers Mindfulness Daily, a downloadable app including forty ten-minute sessions conducted by Tara and Jack Kornfield, author and Buddhist practitioner.

The Oprah & Deepak 21-Day Meditation

I love Oprah! She's partnered with Deepak Chopra to create this easy-to-follow twenty-minute routine. It's offered free a few times a year. After the free run, they are available for sale and can be enjoyed from a pretty app.

Headspace

This is *great* for anyone brand new to meditation. It has an easy, free, ten-day, ten-minute introductory app. I had my son use it while he was handling the grueling schedule of his junior and senior years in high school. He listened to it before he got out of bed. Headspace helped him with writing and being organized. He's continued to use it in college. It's on his phone and easy to access.

Prayer

Prayer was modeled for me by my parents, my grandparents, and by numerous aunts and uncles. We always went to church on Sundays and said grace at dinner. If something bad happened and prayers were needed, my mother even brought us to church before school. My grandmother also loved to pray and talked about the Blessed Mother as if she were her friend. She referred to the Blessed Mother with joy and happiness and was a devotee of the Rosary.

With all these great vibes around prayer, it's no surprise that I love it. I'm relaxed and feel safe when I am praying and I am always looking for ways to become more faithful.

In the summer of 2015, I heard Immaculée Ilibagiza speak for the first time. I was at the National Speakers Association (NSA) Convention seated with about three thousand other people. I was inspired to see this woman standing on stage holding a rosary. She was telling the unbelievable story of her survival of the genocide in Rwanda. I was so happy to see that a woman talking about her devotion to faith and prayer was a sought-after speaker! When I returned to New York, I reached out to Immaculée to get her involved with the NSA activities in New York.

Immaculée and I met for lunch and we shared everything we loved about being mothers, living in New York, and having our own businesses. She made me want to be a better Catholic. Since our meeting, I have made a point of saying the Rosary as often as I can with a goal of four times a week.

Prayer is a daily practice for me done at the same time of the morning as meditation. Some people may separate them or do one instead the other, and that is fine.

What is the outcome of your THINK step?

Meditation and prayer set a tone for the way I feel about my day. I no longer feel like my thoughts are going to give me a heart attack. I increasingly feel less anxious about events messing up my schedule or not happening at all. I know the next minute, hour, day, and week is in front of me. It's helped me to be as present as possible when life's inevitable, unplanned events take me off course.

What is the improv practice associated with THINK?

Enter free of thought. Leave what you know to be true out of "the scene" in your head. We have a lot of information from past events in our heads. We know a lot about patterns with people in our lives and tend to bring those with us when we don't need them. Get out of your head! Actors who enter a space thinking they know which way the scene is going to go are sure to contribute to the scene's demise. Seasoned improvisers enter the scene free of thought. When they do this, surprises ensue and the inevitable outcome is laughter.

The irony of calling this step THINK, when it suggests the opposite, is not lost on me. I would like readers to remember they are always free to think of nothing and that would make a space for something.

What do I still want to improve?

My goal over the next few years is to increase the duration and number of times I meditate in a day. I am looking forward to attending retreats with some of my favorite meditation teachers and to practicing Transcendental Meditation. I'm looking forward to going on a pilgrimage with Immaculée and to Lourdes with my friend, Father Dunn. I also want to take my Rosary practice to a deeper level.

THINK: The Space of YES for ***YOU***

In this section, write what you do when you first wake up.

1. Are you happy with any part of this list? If so, which ones?
2. Would you like to add or improve the spiritual practice you have?
3. Do you have a spiritual role model? What do you like about their practice?
4. What could you do *today* that will help you get where you want to go?

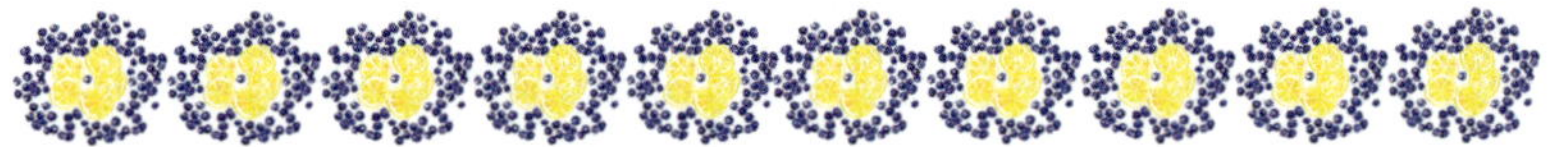

THINK.

The Space of YES for YOU

"Think for yourself and you will move forward. Think for others and you will stay stuck."

"Invite definition into your life by being more definitive."

"Speak of plans, not excuses."

Water

I've had a love affair with water my entire life. Anyone who knows me knows I drink more water in a day than some people drink in a week. I also have visited more restrooms than most people I know. This is a side effect of my love affair with water.

My water usually comes from the filter in my refrigerator. I pour my first glass after I weigh myself and before I meditate.

I take my water with a squeeze of lemon first thing and throughout the day. This is the chance to connect with my five senses and everything going into my mouth. I *smell* the lemon after I cut it and before I squeeze it!

These repeated steps help me to feel connected to the water and to be present for that first glass. This kind of talk may seem a little "crunchy" at first, and I understand that. I'm taking the time to write all these steps so you can see how they are connected to the solid steps you are going to create for yourself.

By smelling the lemon and taking time with the first glass of water, you open up your senses and say YES to your first drink!

A few years ago, I started paying more attention to plants. After my cousin bought me a lemon tree, I decided to tap into my inner gardener. I have about ten plants now (including some herbs and a poinsettia). They all spend the winter inside with me, and most of them go outside in the summer. I'm excited to write about them because I feel successful when I look at them and see how they are thriving. They need me to nurture them. They've helped me to see that the sun and the attention I give them help them to grow—and the thing they need more than anything else is...*water*! If I am behind when it's time to water them, they show their appreciation when I do; they go from wilted to strong in mere hours. This thrills me because it deepens my love for water and my assertion that *we* need water as much as plants do. We can go from wilted to strong with a hearty glass of H_2O.

Other Non-Alcoholic Beverages

In short, focus on drinking liquids with fewer calories and no caffeine. You know this is a good practice. Learn how the drinks you like make you feel. Decide what to keep and what to tweak.

I love coffee. I drink two cups every morning. I used to have *lots* of half-and-half in my coffee, and I realized that had to be cut back. In order to increase my consciousness with the half-and-half, I started measuring it with a teaspoon. That must have been more than five years ago and I've never stopped. I always measure the half-and-half and, as a result, taste and enjoy my coffee more.

Many years ago while coping with sleeping disruptions, I realized if I have *any* caffeine after 2:00 p.m. (including anything with caffeine in it, like chocolate) I will have trouble *staying* asleep once I am asleep. I *love* sleeping. The stress created each time I looked at the clock at 2:30 a.m. was enough of a motivator to figure this out.

When I get off track and drink (or eat) something with caffeine, I wake up in the middle of the night. It's that simple.

Drink before bed

Sleepytime tea is a precious nighttime ritual; I now share this ritual with my children. (This is the actual name of the tea that I like.) Looking forward to this tea has become a substitute for wanting food at night. My son James is a singer. He needed to take care of his voice, so I made a concoction of hot water, honey, lemon, and fresh ginger. He made this tea his nighttime go-to. The act of boiling the water, preparing the mugs with the tea bags, slicing the lemons and ginger, and pouring the honey are all part of the routine. This is a way we can easily show our love for one another when one of us delivers the tea or concoction to the other.

Alcohol:
Adjustment Inspired by Reunion

The year before my twentieth reunion, I was at an event at my college representing my alumnae board. Each class got up on the dais and had their picture taken together. There was a banner showing the year they graduated. When the class celebrating their fiftieth reunion got up, I was taken aback by how different these women looked who were the *same age*! Some looked like they were wearing the weight of the world on their shoulders and some looked closer to their energetic, happy, twenty-something self. Some looked naturally content and others looked worn out. Many of the people lacking energy didn't look healthy and had a harder time moving up the stairs to the dais.

It was at that moment that I told myself I would look like one of the energetic ones by the time I got up there a year later, for my twentieth reunion. I set a goal to lose the weight I needed to lose, and to give myself one year to do it. It was time to take stock and realize that *everything* going into my body was going to look like something *on me* at some point. What were some of the things I was drinking and eating that made me feel energetic? What were some of the things I was drinking and eating that drained me?

One of the most important things I addressed was alcohol. I didn't drink a lot. But more often as I got into my late thirties and early forties, when I did drink, I became foggy faster, and I felt horrible the next day. I came to terms that I was one of those people who can drink but I had to set a solid limit on how much and stick to it.

For my fortieth birthday, I went to Canyon Ranch alone. I highly recommend doing something like this. There was a lot of soul searching I had to do and it was much-needed time *alone*.

It was there that I had a nutritional consult. I confided in the counselor that I had headaches that lasted three days. They were chronic and wore me out. I wasn't sure if they were migraine headaches but they were awful and always lasted three days.

She told me to write down what I ate and drank in a typical week. She suggested I limit or remove red wine to see if the headaches went away. I did that, and it worked; the headaches went away. Through further experimentation, I found that too much chocolate also contributed to these headaches. Don't think for a minute that I gave up chocolate. But I *do* pay more attention to *when* I have it and *how much* I have.

Going through this process helped me create a system I could fall back on that is as reliable as the scale. By your late thirties and early forties, you know what you can handle, what you like and how you want to feel.

The "two" guide

I can have two certain alcoholic drinks and I have them in a special order. Use the workbook portion of the book (after this chapter) to write down what you love to drink. Then write down how you feel when you drink them.

If the number you drink makes you feel drained, then reduce how many you drink. If they still drain you, then consider *what* you are drinking. Consider replacing these drinks with something that makes you less drained.

My number is *two* and I only drink certain wines and cocktails that are on my list. If I go past the "two" guide, then I will feel like rubbish the next day for the entire day. If I feel like rubbish, I will eat more and I will gain weight. If I go past the two to three times a week guide, I can watch the weight come back on. It's that simple. Know the guide and know what happens when you steer away from it.

I invested many words on this topic because it's important to have a handle on it by the time you are fifty.

I recently had someone watch me take a sip of my martini and she said, "Wait! You drink *gin* and you're so thin?" (*Please note, again*: I am not "thin." "Thin" is a word people use when they are proud of you for losing weight. Back to my story...) Then I told her I was having *one*. She said, "Oh, just *one*... yeah, not sure I could do that but I've gotta do something."

When the friend in this story said she had to "do something," I really wanted to meet her where she was and give her a place to start. That is why I use the word "guide," which suggests you are going somewhere. I now think of the two drinks I am going to have as a treat and I hope people who want to "do something" think they have a good place to start.

Improv practice having to do with DRINK

In the THINK section, I aligned with the improv practice of getting out of your head and freely entering the space. This creates openness and intention. Drinking anything is best done with intention. If you are enjoying a cocktail or a glass of wine, then also *enjoy* it and the person you are sharing it with. If you are alone, toast someone. Say YES to having a drink.

What do I still want to improve?

I'm really not sure what I want to improve because I have come a long way in this area. There may be a time when I drink alcohol even less and that would probably be a really good thing.

Your notes

If this portion of the DRINK part of this book is resonating with you, move to the notes section and answer these questions:

1. What do I love about having a drink?
2. How often do I drink?
3. Is paying more attention to this topic something I've been meaning to do?
4. What small step could I take to improve the way I feel about this topic?

When I answered these questions for myself, I realized I loved the drink even before I took a sip. A drink was connected to celebration and time to relax. That's a good thing because it wasn't as if the drink were connected to the mundane. It was connected to celebration and being with others.

DRINK: The Space of YES for YOU

If you feel what you drink is having an adverse effect on your body, then write down how you *want* to feel. You know what you want and only you can create the mindset to accomplish your goal.

This process may take you a few months and maybe it will take you a year. Figure out if what you drink is keeping you from how you want to feel.

Take a look at soda, coffee, tea, and other drinks. I'm not telling you to eliminate them. I'm telling you to write down what they are, how much you love them, and what, if any, side effects they could be adding to your day. How are the side effects affecting how you feel?

DRINK.
The Space of YES for YOU

"More living breeds less longing."

"You know everything you need to know about you; go ahead and access it."

"The best way to attract people who have faith in you is to have faith in yourself first."

This section is about YES foods and NO foods.

When I eat mostly YES foods, I maintain and even sometimes lose weight. When I eat more NO foods, I gain weight. It's that simple.

I train my clients to use YES words so they may communicate more positively. It was also fitting to do so with food references and descriptions.

These YES and NO words keep me on track in other areas where I communicate. Because of that, it seemed fitting to move them to the food descriptions. This way, I always have something to fall back on when I get off track.

I'd weigh at least twenty pounds more if I ate what my teenaged boys ate. So I have a simple strategy. If I am fixing a huge meal for them, I have in place what I will eat. *Most* importantly, I will have already eaten enough throughout the day so I don't feel famished looking at a plate of lasagna or meatballs or beef goulash. This helps me to still enjoy what they are having in the portion that works for me. For example, I'll have a ramekin-sized portion (three-inch ramekin) of what they are eating then fill the rest of my plate with lettuce and veggies. That way I feel like I'm part of their party!
Ramekin: noun: a small dish for baking and serving an individual portion of food.

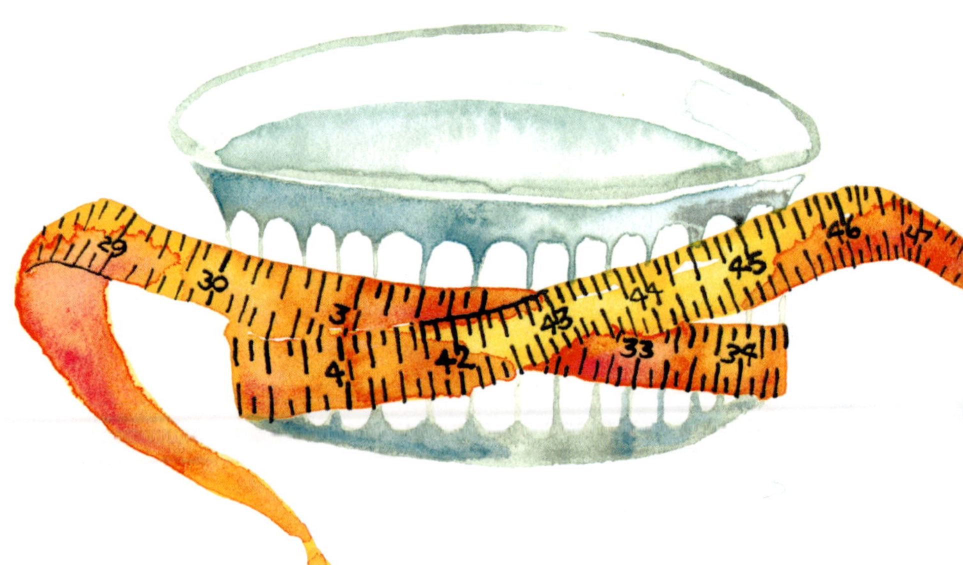

Food shopping routine

Treat the spaces where you buy food like a live improv stage. Your only script is the grocery list. Get out of your head and say "hello" to perfect strangers. Make eye contact while gathering your produce. For example, comment on the fact that the lemons were much cheaper last week or that they moved the cereal display. When you do this, you'll help someone get out of their head while you move through the store. This added exercise is meant to create more harmony with the food you are buying and with this ever-important step to EAT.

Grocery shopping is a great opportunity to develop a relationship with food. The act of grocery shopping and interacting with other people is part of saying YES to the space of food. This leads us to YES foods.

What are YES Foods?

By now you know I love the word YES. I believe that when we understand our YES we can uncover momentum when we are stuck. I love naming my YES foods. It's fun! Why not have fun with food before you even eat it?

YES foods are my friends (like the scale). Calling them "friends" helps to remind us they are there to support us and make us feel good.

My food choices are fun, like my friends are fun. I look forward to what I am going to eat and that kind of thinking helps me enjoy grocery shopping a lot more.

YES Foods

Breakfast

- Fruit (blueberries, strawberries, melon, grapefruit)
- Shredded Wheat cereal

- Skim milk or almond milk
- Oatmeal
- Honey
- Eggs
- Whole wheat toast

The more fruit you put in your cereal or oatmeal, the less oatmeal or cereal you will eat. Over time, this is your goal. Start where you feel comfortable and then focus on the goal of more fruit. Blueberries and strawberries can be easily found in the grocery store all year-round. Melon and grapefruit are good alone and best enjoyed in season. Use just enough milk (or no milk) to cover the cereal or oatmeal. Start where you feel comfortable and work toward this goal. If you really must have a sweetener, honey is best.

Eggs can be eaten anytime. Have one or two with dry whole-wheat toast and prepare them the way you like them. I eat eggs about once or twice a week. They are also a go-to food if I've skipped a meal and I'm famished. They are a satisfying filler. As for butter, start where you want. Your goal is to decrease the amount of butter until you're fine with dry toast. Then you'll see the butter as a "treat" some day. Pick combinations of foods you like and create a routine with them.

I once heard Raquel Welch say she enjoys a hearty snack of three carrots. Her point was, if you want to remain lean, you need to make a conscious decision to eat less. Period. That is why, in this section and in the following two sections, I tell you to start where you feel comfortable. Meet yourself where you are *now* with a goal to decrease your intake.

Lunch

- Lettuce, lettuce, lettuce! (pick your favorite lettuce and fill the plate)
- Oil and vinegar, or no dressing
- Goat cheese (teeny, tiny bit)
- Grilled chicken
- Tuna (white tuna in water, less than 2 tablespoons mayo, tons of chopped celery, and a little chopped onion); eat with Wasa crispbread
- Chickpeas
- Avocado
- Soup (Amy's in a can; lentil or split pea are my favorites)

Eat lettuce *at least* once a day. It's the most reliable, easy-to-keep, and easy-to-assemble roughage around! Salad dressing is a complete waste to me. It's loaded with stuff we don't need and it ultimately keeps me from tasting the lettuce, which I really love. So I am an oil-and-vinegar, salt-and-pepper girl and I've been using less and less (of that) over the years too.

Goat cheese, grilled chicken, or chickpeas are the toppers of my salads. Start with what fills you. Work toward less. Go ahead and make the whole can of tuna and eat it all if you like. The goal is to have some left over for a snack later. Wasa crispbread becomes the most delicious, crunchy thing you've ever tasted.

If you need more filler, chickpeas are an extra treat on top of the salad. They are easy to keep handy for a snack. They can also be roasted at 350 degrees on a cookie sheet, with a drizzle of olive oil and salt and pepper, until slightly browned.

A friend who is a vision of health and happiness was once asked what one of her favorite go-to foods was. She said, "avocado." The person she said it to said, "Oh, I don't really like avocados." My friend said, "Learn to!" Her answer made me laugh and made me consciously keep avocados nestled with my lemons, limes, and apples *all year*. An avocado transforms a great big plate of *lettuce*. It can also be a snack, sliced in half with a drizzle of vinegar, salt, and pepper.

When I visited Canyon Ranch for my fortieth birthday, I *loved* the soup! I ate it every day I was there. The day I was leaving, I asked one of the waitresses if I could have the recipe. She whispered, "It's from a can: Amy's. It's organic and you can buy it in the grocery store." *This* is my go-to soup, along with an occasional chicken broth—simple, easy, stocked and ready to go!

Eating out at restaurants

In almost all restaurants, you can order any salad as you want it, and you can usually count on a simple soup to start the meal. Order entrees without the carbs and ask for double the veggies. At work lunches and dinners, when I'm engrossed in conversation I usually eat a lot less. That means you can take your leftovers to eat later. Also, I'm drinking *a lot* of water during these restaurant meals, which keeps me from eating more.

Dinner

- Lettuce, lettuce, lettuce, and more lettuce (did I mention lettuce?)
- Salmon, grilled or baked with a simple low-salt seasoning and lemon

- Flounder, with breadcrumbs made from grated whole wheat toast, drizzled over the fish with two sliced lemons and pats of butter, baked at 350 degrees F until the breadcrumbs are slightly browned
- Steak, grilled with salt and pepper
- Soft tacos—your goal is to eat only two and to keep sauces to a minimum

Veggies

- Asparagus, sautéed with butter, enough to make the pan shine and heated enough to stay bright green under the pan cover
- Brussels sprouts, tops sliced off and cut in half, tossed with olive oil, salt, and pepper, and baked on a cookie sheet at 400 degrees F until golden brown
- Sweet potatoes, baked at 400 degrees F until soft, peel off the skin, and mash
- Broccoli, sautéed in a pan with garlic or shallots and olive oil
- Broccoli rabe, same as broccoli
- Green beans, same as broccoli

The best dinners include a little protein and a lot of veggies. In short, I've greatly reduced carbs. I eat them—I just don't eat them as much anymore and I steer clear of them later in the day. This is now a new habit and because of that it's a rare event that I crave them at all.

I love almost all veggies. The more of them I eat, the better I feel and the higher my energy. It is on my list to become a "juicer." When I do, I am sure I will be able to take my veggie devotion to a whole new level.

Eating every two to three hours

Eating every two to three hours may be the best practice of all. By doing this, I may have shrunk my stomach. I cannot prove this but I can tell you that I now become full *very* fast. Also, because of the routine I observe with snacks (see the following), I'm really satisfied with what I eat, and when I eat.

Snacks

- Apples (I *love* Honeycrisp all year), melons, grapefruits, oranges
- Nut mix—fill a ramekin with roasted, unsalted almonds (15 or less), jumbo raisins (a smaller portion than the almonds), and unsalted, raw pumpkin seeds. You may create any combination you like, but this is my favorite. Over the years, I figured out which dried fruits "agree" with me and which do not. I also realized the less salt, the better. I make this in advance and put it into baggies. I can grab it and have in my pocketbook when it's time for my snack!
- Triscuits (6 crackers)
- Wheat Thins (16 crackers)
- Carrots (as many as you want)
- Celery (as much as you want)
- Cucumber (as much as you want)

The nut mix has become such a gift. It feels like magic because it's not a lot of food but it really fills me up. I keep the nut mix in my pocketbook. It's a complete relief when I need to eat something and I'm away from a source for good choices.

The Triscuits and Wheat Thins make me very happy. They are my "go-to" carbs. I count them and put them in a ramekin.

My son Harry recently watched me counting and said, "Did you get to 16 yet?" I love that he shares my routine!

Having this in my head keeps me from feeling out of control. When my life is not simple, this menu is easy to fall back on. Ultimately I feel successful and lighter. I feel like I own something no one can take away from me.

Measuring

You may have noticed I don't really talk about calories or too many measurements. We have enough on our minds and measuring can be daunting and depressing. When you establish a goal of packing your plate with YES foods and realize the power of veggies, you feel less mopey and look at a ramekin-sized portion as a serving size. Ramekins are pretty and they don't have numbers on them!

Do I ever go off the plan?

Yes! Because I practice the preceding routine with food choices, I have room to have fun and go off the plan. Having fun feels better when you've made the space for it.

Food Summary

What you've read here is my go-to menu. It's simple and easy to accomplish. This feels like a relief because sometimes I am overwhelmed by all the other decisions I have to make.

Communicating with children about food

While they are eating breakfast, the first words out of teenaged boys are, "What's for dinner?" This question used to make me crazy and I learned to get ahead of that feeling of being overwhelmed. I created a plan for four out of seven nights when I am likely cooking. On Sunday night I'll say, "Monday is chicken cutlets, Tuesday is salmon, Wednesday is pasta, and Thursday is meatballs and spaghetti." They love this and stay quiet without any further questions. Even if I change what is being made on a particular day, it matters little to them. They have heard the answer to their most burning question. They know I have their backs and that there is a plan in place for their food.

This is an important lesson in communication and in improv. Know your audience and meet them where they are. My children have food on their minds more often than not. Rather than resent that their mindset means work for me, I now embrace it as one of those things that connects us—eating together.

This helps me to feel better about grocery shopping, cooking, and cleaning it all up!

Sugar/Candy/Dessert

Twice a month, I used to treat myself to an ice cream soda with Häagen-Dazs coffee ice cream and Stewart's diet root beer (yes, diet). It was quite a ritual, and I ate every drop. This was a full-blown Jeanne-party and a treat. I had as much as I wanted because I would be back on track the next day.

I created structure for my treat by scheduling it twice a month. I was meeting myself "where I was" and made it my intention to decrease from there. It worked because now it's rare for me to eat dessert even as part of a ritual. It's pretty much for a special occasion or if I am tempted to taste something my men are eating. If my children go out for ice cream and they've chosen something I like, I'll put some in—you guessed it—a ramekin!

The daily handful

On the sugar front, the last thing I had to conquer was my daily handful. I had a need for sugar, a pang, as it were, and it happened at around 2:00 p.m.–3:00 p.m. every day. I made the treat acceptable by taking a handful or a ramekin full. My sugars of choice were black licorice, Jujyfruit candy, a piece of chocolate, or a cookie (or two). While I had no desire to completely eliminate sugar from my life, I did want to address my need for a daily sugar fix.

My friend Immaculée told me how easy it is to manifest what we want. She told me to find something I thought I needed and to practice having a quiet moment of prayer in place of it.

That was my opportunity to address the daily handful. When that time of the day came, I marched over to the cabinet with the goodies in it, paused, and prayed for what I would like to have happen instead of eating. (Please note: I am a *big* dreamer and I pray *big*. When what I prayed for comes true, I will let you know.)

When we pray, I also know that sometimes we receive gifts we may not have been looking for. My grandmother used to say, "Don't miss it because it didn't come packaged the way you wished for it." My grandmother was *brilliant*, and her words also made sense to my inner improviser. In an improv scene, most of the greatest events are unplanned.

The result of this practice, suggested by Immaculée, caused me to lose five pounds in a very short time. It basically eliminated "the daily handful."

For special occasions, I eat dessert and, when the time calls for it, I'll partake in the sugar and candy party. As of today, my daily handful has been replaced with my nut mix. The sugar stash in my cabinet is gone and not missed!

Improv practice having to do with EAT

When an audience (watching an improv show) figures out the relationships the characters have with one another, they feel satisfied. In the nineteen years I have been studying improv, one teacher in particular drives this home more than any other. When my short-form improv teacher, Ralph Buckley, is teaching a workshop, he gets pretty riled up when the improvisers delay getting to the relationship of the characters. After we have completed a scene in class, he'll ask for questions, comments, and feedback. If there was something in particular that bothered him it will usually have to do with *relationship*. To him, it is the most obvious thing we need to *get to* as improvisers, and he's furious when we miss the chance to do it—*again*. So he says, "What did it need? What was missing?" Then he'll say—really loudly and with his whole self, "*Relationship—relationship—relationship!*"

So the improv practice I would like to associate with EAT is relationship. Your relationship with food is *key* and it's a reflection of the relationships you have with all the people in your life.

Start now with a solid, easily identifiable relationship with your food and it will be easier to move all your scenes forward.

What do I still want to improve with EAT?

I'd like to take more time to eat. I'd like to get better at chewing more and slowing down when I eat. Although I've achieved balance with my food choices I still have work to do with eating slowly. Stay tuned!

EAT: The Space of YES for YOU

Here are some questions to ask yourself.

1. What do you eat now?
2. What is easy for you to assemble and keep on hand?
3. How do you feel when you eat?
4. Is there something you have a ritual around that you would like to eliminate?

Remember to meet yourself where you are while having an idea of where you want to be.

EAT.

The Space of YES for YOU

"Trust yourself and you will enjoy your experiences more completely."

"The best way to teach new behaviors is to model them."

"Trust that the experiences in your life are leading you to connection with your life."

Walking

"I always see you walking, Jeanne." That is something said to me often. I *love* to walk. I walk for forty-five minutes, five to seven days a week. I would like to walk seven days a week but sometimes something gets in the way. And, of course, there are weeks when I don't even get to five times. But I know the practice of repeating positive thoughts to myself will get me back on track. I forgive myself and move to the next opportunity to walk.

This has become so automatic that few things stop me. Too much rain might stop me; I say "too much" because I will walk in mild rain. Too much snow might stop me; I say "too much" because, after landing in some massive drifts, I realized how focused I am on getting out. That's how much snow I need to stop me. By repeating the mantra "Walk five to seven days," I am creating an intention that works past obstacles like weather.

Once you get the exercise or walk underway, transfer your thoughts. A way to become more present for your walk (or any exercise) is to give it to someone, to walk in the name of someone else. For example, I walk for people who can't walk and would love to—some of them I know and some of them I don't know. The simple act of being able to walk is a gift. Being able to move is a gift. When we intentionally devote our exercise to someone else, it reminds us of all the ways there are to give.

I *love* my walk because it *feels* like a gift. I walk without any technology, leaving my phone at home. I want to free myself of thoughts that come with selecting music, checking emails, or answering the phone. This helps me to practice being truly present. That way I have the chance to say hello to my people in Heaven and mindfully dedicate the walk to someone who can't walk.

In the past, I dabbled in kickboxing and spinning. There was a time when I ran. I also have been a student of hot yoga and regular yoga. I replaced these activities with the easiest thing I could initiate at any time. I turned to walking when my resources adjusted and my time shifted. I've realized that this walk I take is a good balance to eating. The kickboxing and spinning left me *famished*. After these classes, I could not stop eating! A walk seems to work well with my metabolism and the amount of food I plan to eat in a day.

My walk is very satisfying because I have a route I love and I look forward to going on it. It's fun to notice the change of seasons and what trees and plants peak first.

My grandmother's favorite poem was *Trees* by Joyce Kilmer, and my favorite line in the poem is:

A tree that looks at God all day,
and lifts her leafy arms to pray;

This line reminds me to look up when I'm walking and take in the size and persevering nature of the trees I see. This helps me to be fully present when I *move*.

Sleep

Think of the choice to sleep as something you *move* to do. Sleep needs to be in this category because it is your choice to move to sleep. When we sleep, we rebuild ourselves so we are stronger to *move* the next day.

Set a goal to make sure your sleep is restoring you.

- Do you like your bed?
- Is your room free of clutter?
- Are your sheets and comforters cozy?
- Does your room smell good?

Sleep needs to be something you look forward to and that you do with increased efficiency.

In the DRINK section, I talked about a time when I used to wake at 2:30 a.m. and was tortured by it. I figured out that certain drinks, the times I drank, and the amounts I drank were the cause of my wakefulness. In addition, I figured out that certain foods affected my sleep too. I made the changes I needed to solve this problem. Now, waking in the middle of the night is a rare event for me. I'm sleeping with increased effortlessness.

The Phone—Off!

Our cellphones have a lot to do with how efficiently we move. When we move well, we want to do it fully. So, when we move to exercise or sleep, we want to be fully present. If the phone is close to you and *on*, this is harder to accomplish.

The phone does *not* belong next to your head when you are sleeping. If you use it as an alarm clock, make sure all other beeps, pings, and noises are *off*! My recommendation is that your cellphone is *not* in your room and that you use something else to wake you up, for example, an alarm clock.

To me, there is nothing more ridiculous than the phone next to your head when you're sleeping. How can you possibly relax? How can you possibly turn your head off enough to sleep? With the phone next to your head, some of the things you can think about are:

1. Why hasn't he texted me back?
2. Did anyone like my post?
3. What's the latest news update on that horrible event?
4. Did that sale start yet?

If you are thinking these things, then you can't prepare yourself for the sleep you deserve. *Turning off* the phone is an exercise in trust and faith. When you do this, you are trusting that you know what you need to know for now. You know that a better night's sleep is worth turning off the phone for. Each time you do this, you are deepening your faith and working toward believing all is well.

When I talk to audiences about this, I am always blown away by the look of relief on the faces in front of me. It seems like they are getting these tips for the first time and that a big weight has been lifted.

The movement of your head and heart to sleep is a precious one. This movement deserves your complete attention.

This practice is the same as the others. Meet yourself where you are and increase the amount of time the phone is turned off, a good hour or more before you fall to sleep. My family and friends know if they need to talk to me about something important, they need to call me before 9:30 p.m. My phone is generally *off* by 9:30.

Of course, there are exceptions. There are times when my phone is left on. There are times when I need to be "on call" for someone who needs me. When that time comes, I know I'm more fully present because all the other nights I practice having it off. I've taken care of myself, so I am ready to take care of others when they *really* need me.

What is the improv practice associated with MOVE?

Walking, attention to sleep, and the act of turning off the phone all *transform* me into someone more calm and present than I was before. Characters in an improv show are very interesting to the audience when they transform. They are different at the end of the scene than they were at the beginning.

Improving the way you move makes room for transformations in your life and for transformations of the character within you. It makes space for unexpected things to happen. Some of the best ideas for my speaking and writing come after I have walked or had a great sleep.

Please note that this fourth category, MOVE, is like the first category, THINK. They both have to do with the spaces you enter with your body and mind. They can be done together, and they are both *free*.

What do I still want to improve with MOVE?

My goal is to take a pilgrimage and to walk and walk and walk. I have a few in mind and will be giving that gift to myself someday. I also want to re-engage with practicing yoga. I stretch every day using the things I've learned after years of yoga. When I am able to add to my MOVE, I will add more yoga: hot yoga and lots of other forms.

As for sleep, I am looking to increase the number of days I get to sleep earlier and wake up earlier.

MOVE: The Space of YES for YOU

1. How do you MOVE now? Do you enjoy it?
2. Are you able to do it as often as you want to?
3. Do you feel connected to the space you do it in?
4. Do you move to sleep well?

Consider the questions in the MOVE section as you write about your practice now. You have new spaces to enter every day. They are *yours* to uncover and move within. Being able to MOVE is a gift. Enjoy this gift you give to yourself.

MOVE.

The Space of YES for YOU

"Give without measure or announcement."

"Step out of your comfort zone today, then twice tomorrow and three times the next day. Record how it feels when you do so mindfully."

"Make time for wandering and wondering."

SUMMARY

Ready, Set, Go!

After you've made your notes and met yourself where you are, give yourself four weeks to create a routine. There are more journaling pages at the end of this book to keep track of your success and to define for yourself what you want when you Think, Drink, Eat, and Move. The goal is to reach next year feeling strong about your mind and body and feeling more at peace overall.

"Can you believe how fast that was?"

We say this every New Year's when we look back on the last year. Apply that same sense to your commitment to Think,

Drink, Eat, and Move yourself to something new. Next year will be here before you know it!

How do you want to look and feel a year or even six months from now? Is what you are doing at this time helping you to get there? If not, is there something inside of you that's ready to let *you* lead the way?

As I wrap up this book, a new school year is here. One son is packing to go to college and the other is on the football field practicing for his fall season. A new beginning has presented itself.

My sons are always ready for every change of season and for each new start. They inspire me with plans for their fantasy football groups and excitement over what times gym and *lunch* are scheduled into their day. They make it all seem so simple.

I'm reflecting on the great order a school year offers us as I pack my James's trunk to go off to college. I also reflect on all the time that has passed. I have come full circle to continue the writing of my next book referenced in the introduction.

When I get the new school calendar, it all looks so neat and orderly. The reality is that the amount of work it takes to balance the lives of family and children can be overwhelming. It can be hard to focus on *you*.

How can we make room for *how* we want to feel?

Perhaps you can look at the four steps to Think, Drink, Eat, and Move as simply as you look at the four seasons in a year. Keep it simple.

In Closing

A big part of me can't believe I wrote this book, shared this personal information, and opened up about a topic that could belong to another writer. It was not easy to cross the line. I doubted myself each time I wrote a sentence, but I played over and over again in my head the voices of the people who'd asked me for this guidance. I kept writing.

In improv, there's nothing funnier and more entertaining than the truth. The truth is what audiences want to hear and then they laugh! Sometimes truth releases laughter, which is a relief. I hope that as I shared my truth, you are able to uncover some relief with what you want to accomplish about how you feel.

When we share truthfully *how* we've uncovered success, we help others uncover theirs. I know after all the jobs I've held, places I've shared my talents as a volunteer, and moments I've experienced as a mother, everyone really wants to be helpful. Most of us forget we can be the most helpful when we model something positive.

Positivity and thinking YES in an improv show move an audience to laugh. Positivity practiced in real life moves people to something new.

I hope that you uncover something new and that, from this day forth, you understand more about the power of YES in YOU than you did before.

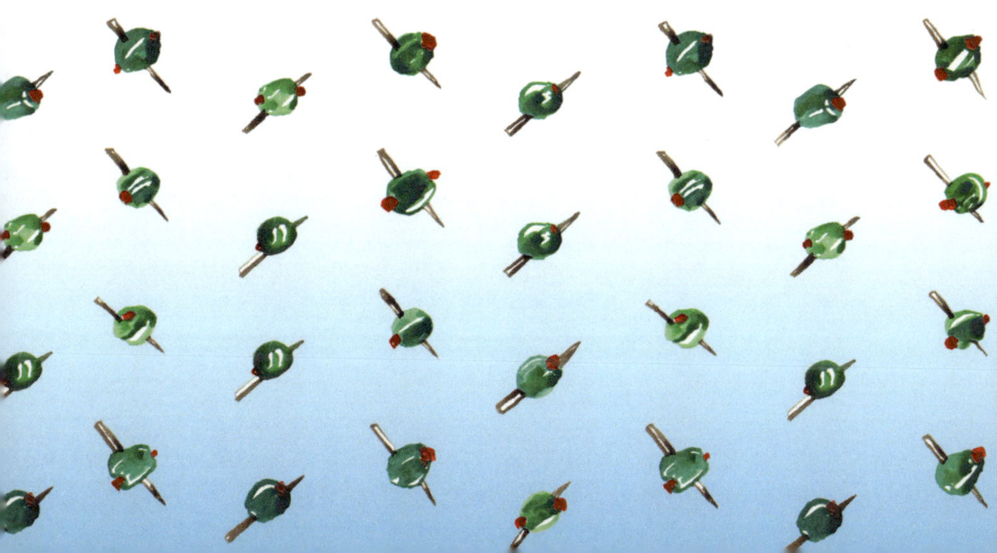

THANK YOU

I would like to thank God for putting me here at this time in this space and for giving me my children, James and Harry. With them in my life I am able to discover so much more about what I am here to do for *you*.

I would like to thank the Blessed Mother for being the model of my favorite job and for the gift of the Rosary so that I may have a place to uncover relief when this job feels too daunting.

I would like to thank my parents for creating a loving, beautiful, safe home with (more) love and food and comfort, and for raising five children who like one another.

I would like to thank my siblings for being models of humor and perseverance, the combination of which I rarely see in one family.

I would like to thank my grandparents—Mommy Kay and Pa (in heaven)—for regularly showing me what joy and fun look like and for being my first unconditionally devoted audience.

I would like to thank my friends and extended family who I'm grateful to say are many in number. You know who you are. You have shown me many paths I would have left uncovered without you in my life.

I would like to thank Robert A. George for being my dear friend in politics, improv and writing. I am grateful for his immeasurable guidance and support as I write and write and write again.

I would like to thank James and Harry, my princes. Because of you I feel safe to go deeper and to love more completely. You have taught me the simple sweetness of being still to better take you both in.

THE POWER OF YES IN YOU

I love writing in the books I read. It's always been important for me to be able to highlight, underline and write out what I am feeling right on the page as I am reading.

When I journal, I've always enjoyed choosing a book to write in with quotes, mantras which act as a positive guide with my sharing.

In this section of the book as my readers chart their way forward I wanted to share some of my favorite blogs. I write a blog on my website which is inspired by a single word and I have been a contributor to the *Huffington Post* and have shared my most popular posts from there. It is my prayer that by reading these posts you gather a little extra energy in your journey to YES.

Enjoy them. Continue to mark up the pages and have fun with this 4-week process of uncovering *more* space of YES for YOU!

Week One: Day One

Care (from my blog, June 14, 2018)

Who takes care of you?

Most of us have a tough time answering this. Most of us know who we take care of but not who takes care of us.

This may be because the answer is so simple, it's hard to imagine it's true.

The person who takes care of you is you.

It is possible to train yourself to understand that you have enough power to take care of your greatest and most immediate needs.

When you train yourself to do this you'll remove years worth of stress and fatigue. This includes the stress and fatigue built up from the past and the stress and fatigue lurking in your thoughts about the future.

You can become an expert at your care and then someday, when it's time to ask for it from someone else you will do so with very little effort. You will be able to do so from a place of inner power instead of that of a victim who has never been cared for.

This year I had to ask for a lot more care than I have ever had to ask for and it was the most unnatural and uncomfortable thing to go through. This was time for Jeanne to learn something new. What I learned was it's easier to receive from others when you have learned to give to yourself.

Caring for yourself is how we get better at communicating what we want from the world and getting it! The result is that more people want to help us, care for us and learn from us.

There are plenty of opportunities to make this important change. These are my four steps to get there. Why four steps? Because I love the number four and when I use it in any strategy, I feel like I am focused. It's a way of caring for myself by simplifying my thoughts. See how easy that was?

Four Steps to Your Daily Caring Strategy

1. Write down the things you want to make easier. Make the list short. What do you want to make easier? Is it streamlining the format for how you create content like the example I gave above? Would you like to get that bank app to make check deposits easier? Do you want to set a reminder on your phone to take a five-minute break? Do you want to get up earlier so you can start the day with a mediation or prayer or have time to read or time to write?
2. Connect with your *intention* behind the step for your care. Will creating your own rules for writing help you deliver better content faster? (My answer is YES to that). Will getting up earlier help you to feel more productive? Communicating intention helps to deepen the trust you have in your own decision-making. When it comes to trust, the trust you have in *you* is the most important trust you can have.
3. Celebrate *any* success you have. If you accomplish anything tell yourself how proud you are when you consciously get this done. If this is less than what you hoped for, shorten the list. You have *enough* on your plate and this is the reason that caring for yourself is on your mind. You have the power to shorten your list, so exercise your power!
4. Tell someone you adore what you are doing and how you *feel*. See if they want to get on the care bandwagon, too. I'll bet they'll say…YES!

Write, Connect, Celebrate and Tell! Those are four things you can do easily and then by the end of summer when someone asks who cares for you, your answer will be simple. "Me!"

Week One: Day Two

Ego (from my blog July 10, 2017)

Your ego is made up of what you know about you, holding memories of both good and bad events, and of people who have disappointed you and people with which you've shared joy. The ego can hold a lot of information and can keep us stuck when we're communicating. The ego looks to control things. It's got all this information and thinks it can fix things.

Clients often tell me, "I want to get her to…" "I need him to…" "We can reward this team when they finally…"

In an improv workshop a few weeks ago, two of my fellow improvisers provided a great example of how we can address this. The first improviser walked into the scene and holding her cheek (looking like she was in pain) and said, "The dentist was a killer…"

The second actor heard something different and said, "The dentist was killed?"

As the actor holding her cheek was about to correct her and say, "No, that's not what I said," the director whispered…

"Say YES…"

When she said "yes" the second line was, "YES! I was sitting in the chair and some crazy person walked in and killed him! Now my mouth is a mess because he couldn't finish!"

We howled! It was a lot funnier to hear the unexpected outcome rather than hear someone steer the scene with the exchange she planned.

This is your ego in *your* exchanges with others. Ego drives us to govern the scenes we enter in our lives. When we do this we miss the opportunity to see something new.

When clients tell me "I want her to…I need him to…this team really needs to…" I ask them to consider what they're missing while they wait for what they want.

Whether you like it or not, your ego it is part of you. There is a way for you to communicate with your ego and direct it more often than it directs you.

Three ways to Say YES and move past your Ego:

1. Trust the Silence. When we get what we want, we're satisfied. When we wait for what we want, we're frustrated. Learn to trust that the time in between things happening is there to build the trust you have in you and the people in your orbit.
2. Re-evaluate top tasks. If people around you are not delivering, maybe you need to communicate a simpler list and/or simpler desired outcomes. Simple is the key word here. You may not need what you think you need.
3. Know what you fear. Your ego is trying to control your exposure to the things you fear. When you know what you fear, you'll be more mindful in the spaces where fear presents itself. This is a great time to pause before you speak and take in what you need to learn.

It's natural to have a strong ego. You'll become an agile communicator when you're aware of how your ego leads. You'll generate interest by the people around you because you'll sound open. You'll be encouraging. You'll be approachable.

You may end up *fixing* yourself and attracting more than you imagined *fixing* would produce!

Week One: Day Three

Growing (from my blog April 25, 2017)

Recently, my cousin returned from a weekend away with some of her closest friends and when I asked her how it was, she said, "It was perfect." I asked what made it perfect, she said, "We're all still growing." "Still growing" was the equivalent of perfect. I couldn't agree more.

This is the time of year when things grow right before our eyes. I have a lemon tree and I realized in December it didn't look as robust as the lemon trees I was seeing in pictures. Some of the leaves were turning brown and there weren't as many lemons popping up. My lemon tree wasn't growing the way it should.

When I researched the problem I discovered it needed more direct sun than I was giving it and that when I watered it, I needed to saturate the soil a few inches down. So I have started loosening up the soil before watering and moved the plant into direct sun.

The change in only a month with the new location and new watering routine is remarkable. More buds for leaves and even a few flower buds.

It's growing!

That's how we grow. We replant. Look at things from a different perspective and change the way we take in physical and mental nourishment. Consider the proverbial leaves on your tree. Do you feel the way you want to feel? Are new things coming out of you? Are you feeling you could grow faster?

Communication is the first place we can start to uncover all the ways we can grow.

Start by asking yourself...

Am I communicating in a way that makes it easy for people to communicate with me? Am I communicating in ways that express my wants and needs? Am I communicating in a way that has a positive effect on those in both my professional and personal life?

With clients in my Communications Training we focus on:

- What to say
- How to speak up
- When to listen

You know you're on the path to growing when…

You speak of plans, not excuses.

You have realizations, not regrets.

You understand where you've been and regularly make room for where you are going.

My cousin discovered this perfect moment while she was with friends she loved on a vacation together. This is a signal that sometimes we need to get out of our space to re-discover what is growing. You can find the better place to grow within yourself. You don't need to buy anything or even move much. Your version of perfect (like my cousin's) may be closer than you thought.

Week One: Day Four

Offer (from my blog, January 11, 2017)

Christmas Eve morning I woke up at 4:30 from a *great* dream. My subconscious was so active that when I woke up I felt like I was finishing an actual conversation I was having in real time and I felt really motivated.

I dreamt that Lin-Manuel Miranda, the creator of "Hamilton" The Musical (as if I need to tell you who he is) called to say he'd like to be a speaker at my networking dinner.

He was kind and humble and really interested because he'd heard about the event from a friend and, initially, I thought he was calling to talk about his friend being a guest speaker. The details on who the friend was (in the dream) were shaky but his desire to communicate with me about my event was clear and by the end of the call it felt like we'd become great friends.

Then I woke up.

I'm sharing my dream to illustrate that great offers are presented to us in every space we enter and it happens to you too. In an improv scene, an "Offer" is something the improviser recognizes and uses to help them move the scene forward. Something new and often funny is created.

I saw the dream as an offer and as a result I assembled a list of people I would like to advise and work with to deliver keynotes, workshops and have as guest speakers for my dinners.

How can you spot an offer?

- Offers are unexpected and when they first present themselves you might think, "I'll do that later" or "That's crazy."
- The offers—that are the most valuable—come to you from people you really like and admire and when they first happen, you often feel separate or unworthy of the next move.

What happens when you say YES to offers?

- You learn to get outside of your comfort zone more often—where you want to be as often as possible—because you *grow* outside your comfort zone.
- You receive the invitations you want from more new people.
- You end up saying YES to less because you've learned to receive only the offers you need for now. Interactions are easier because you've increased your confidence and are communicating more clearly what value you have to offer.

While my conversation with Lin-Manuel Miranda happened in my dream—and not in real life—it's helped me to be alert to what is in front of me. It motivated me to take action and think bigger than what I'd originally planned.

My hope is that hearing about the offer I received helps you to wake up to possibilities in front of you. Let this be *your YES year!*

Week One: Day Five

Simple (from my blog, December 19, 2016)

We are all very different and yet, we all want the same things. We want to be happy and feel successful. Getting to this seems much harder than it's ever been before.

We're having a hard time because there are more places than ever to communicate.

We're posting, emailing, texting, talking on our phones. We're communicating with loved ones, professional networks, new friends, old friends, people with shared interests and different opinions.

Then we become overwhelmed and stuck. When we are stuck, we cannot move forward.

As I enter my sixth year hosting Jeanne Stafford's Networking Dinner, I realize this event has become important to people. The feedback I receive is how great it *feels* to be in a live space, to meet people, hear from a diverse spectrum of guests and speakers and talk about what matters to us.

It's become an extension of my workshops and keynotes and a space *anyone* can join.

To help my guests to become unstuck, I shared three steps to achieve momentum in conversations at home, at work *and* on social media. That last one seems to be causing the greatest amount of stress for my clients.

3 Steps to Simple Communication

1. Be Consistent

   Know what you want to communicate and be consistent with those messages. When you consistently communicate simple messages, people learn what you are about and the people you want in your life arrive.

2. Be Resistant

    It's tempting to engage in communication about things outside of our focus especially the things we see on Facebook, Twitter and Instagram—we know the messenger and/or the topic may tug at our hearts. Resist this temptation and you will increase your ability to get back on track and be a more disciplined communicator.

3. Be *Free*

    The opposite of freedom is imprisonment and our thoughts can keep us imprisoned. When you train yourself to let go of the things that you are bothered by, you are free to see more of the opportunities in front of you. Most of the things holding us back are memories about where we've been and what went wrong when we were there.

To enter a space free of thoughts from the past and free from wants of the future—is to be free.

You can get there with patience, discipline and devotion to this practice of simplicity—and the larger practice of saying YES!

Week One: Day Six

Formula (from my blog, October 26, 2016)

I am often asked how I grew such a network of people and how I get the speakers for my networking dinners and the clients I have the honor to train? How did I land the Chief of Global Human Resources for a Fortune 500 company or a world famous actress to be the guest speakers for my dinner? How did I get to coach a three-star general in the Marine Corps as he transitioned in his leadership role?

"What's your formula, Jeanne?"

The answer: I seek relationships, not outcomes.

Our outcome-seeking culture may tell you that this is a bad formula because it doesn't always yield immediate results. From my own experiences, the promise of immediate results doesn't last over the long haul.

It is the long haul I am most invested in.

For my training methods with both individuals and teams, improv has provided a foundation for formulas that work. An audience watching a show feels engaged as soon as they understand and feel the relationship of the characters. We were made to go deeper and feel more fully when we work. Relationships are key to the stories we watch when we watch improv.

In our real lives, relationships are key and they take time to cultivate.

I never stop connecting. The most solid forces in my work and personal life are also relentless connectors. We understand and nurture this powerful group.

Everyone reading this can get real results when making someone feel good. People will remember how you made them feel which will pay off over time.

Jeanne's 3 Steps to Build Relationships For Results

1. Practice Pro-Active Communication

If you see an article or hear a story that reminds you of someone you know and want to get to know better, email them, private message them, share it with them via Twitter or LinkedIn and quote them—*always*. When I do this I am thanked for my kindness and for thinking of them.

2. Be patient with people if you don't hear back

If someone is not responding to your email and/or a call and your instinct told you that you've got a solid connection with this person, trust your instinct and *never* give up on reaching out to them. Give it a few weeks or months and reach out again with positivity and pick up where you left off when you last connected. I cannot tell you how many people I have done this with who have thanked me for my persistence. Do this only when you are sure there was a solid connection at your initial meeting.

3. Give without measure or announcement

When you practice the above two steps remember giving is giving and when we give well we do so without seeking something in return. This idea really smacks in the face of most outcome seekers because it is thought we must want something in return. What I have learned is that when I give without measure or announcement what I receive is better and richer than what I would have imagined as an outcome.

Week One: Day Seven

Conversation (from my blog, July 26, 2016)

The messages of conflict presented to us in the news every day may keep us from feeling like we have control over what happens in our lives. Now more than ever, we need to uncover ways to communicate successfully.

I said YES to an invitation to speak alongside the former president of Planned Parenthood, Gloria Feldt. The event was held by the founder of the 6 Figures Network, Jan Mercer Dahms, who wanted to start a conversation about how women can play a more significant role in politics.

Gloria and I knew we would like each other, despite not agreeing politically. We had both been in numerous situations where we had to communicate in the face of adversity about our cause. We were both experienced at staying on message despite anything being thrown our way.

Over fifty professional New York City women were present at this interactive talk. The last guest given the chance to ask a question decided instead to give us feedback. She said, "I want to thank you because I just listened and watched as the two of you had a conversation. With everything going on in the political discourse today, I did not come here expecting that. Thank you for showing us that it can be done."

My work is complete!

That is what good, solid, positive, proactive communication is. Making the space to learn something new and realizing with great humility that when we do this, we will be transformed, feeling better both about ourselves and others.

That is why I am a devotee of YES and committed to training others at seeing their YES. When we stay connected to what we are here to do, then we are better at staying on message and enjoying conversations even when they are with people from different backgrounds and beliefs.

Week Two: Day One

Time (from my blog, July 7, 2016)

There are events in life that present themselves over and over again and there are events in life that happen only once.

This past month, I watched my oldest son graduate from high school and attend his college orientation.

These milestones went off without a hitch and it took a lot of work to get there. Two months ago when I looked at the calendar and the crunch of events happening at the same time, I felt sick to my stomach. Then I decided to take matters into my own hands.

I decided to make time for this time.

As I prepared to enjoy the graduation and orientation and the events surrounding both, I took steps to re-direct meetings and tended less to the things I usually do in an ordinary week (although I don't think I've ever had an "ordinary" week).

I knew I needed to be present for the actual events. I knew I needed to carve out the time to process all the emotions.

In my training sessions, clients constantly tell me they need more time, they are strapped for time and what they need is time. When they say it, they seem exhausted and it's always my goal to frame "Time" for them in a way that gives them control.

Consider these simple steps when you feel stressed about your time:

1. Put the phone *down—off—out of sight* as often as you are able. When you are looking for your phone to give you the feedback you are giving your time and power away.

2. Get up earlier—this is your chance to feel better about your time. This becomes a form of self-care and when practiced regularly can feel like a mini vacation. Later in the day you will feel less resentment about the time you need to give to others because you will have created time for yourself earlier in the day.

3. Put the *to-do* list down. It will always be there. When you want to make time for important events and people in your life, focus on one thing at a time. We often multi-task because we think we can do it all when in fact, the best way to *feel* good about our time is to focus on what we want from it.

We have twenty-four magnificent hours presented to us every day and a new moment arrives every second. Our time belongs to us and it takes remembering that.

Time is yours to love and to live fully!

Week Two Day Two

Sorry (from my blog, April 15, 2016)

I recently had a meltdown and caused a scene in front of my children in reaction to something their father—my former significant other—said to me.

I am not proud of the way I yelled and lost my temper. I am not proud of how long it took me to pull myself together.

Even though I planned on keeping this little episode to myself, I decided to invite my readers into this event because I went from feeling so awful about it to feeling much better about it after I said, "I'm sorry."

It took me a day of cooling down before I could use the "S" word. I was sure of all the reasons I was right for being mad. I reviewed them in my head and knew I had cause for feeling hurt enough to express it. I did not have cause for blowing up the way I did. That was wrong.

When I apologized, I did so by saying how sorry I felt for losing my cool and for making everyone so upset. Then I clearly stated what set me off and why.

When an actor leaves an improv scene they need to be different than they were at the beginning of the scene. They need to transform in order to present a pleasing story for the audience.

I needed to show my audience—my children—what it looked like to accept responsibility for my actions and be affected by the events enough to know I needed to apologize.

By saying I was sorry, I experienced outcomes of relief.

It is a lot easier to discuss new things I needed to discuss with my former significant other after clearing the air.

I felt less anguish about the thing that set me off when I blew up. Miraculously, I actually have trouble at this moment remembering what it was.

Since I make it my business to help people navigate conflict it's important to share how I've done it in my own life.

We all need a little relief sometimes. I learned from this scene that all the relief was mine for the asking. All the relief was mine with a simple word. Sorry.

Week Two: Day Three

Love (from my blog, February 13, 2016)

You can love anything. You can love a day of the week, you can love a particular kind of food, you can love a song and you can love a sound. You can love anything.

Love is available to you in every space you enter. I encourage my clients to tap into the way they feel about the simple things they love as often as they are able.

When you know what you love and why you love it, you better understand what you want from the life you are living, work you are doing and people you are doing it with.

This time of year, the message is that love is best and truest when it is shared with a romantic partner. I believe that kind of love emerges more fully and completely when we have achieved an understanding of ourselves.

When I work with teams of people the biggest transformations happen in the room when we talk about what we love. They usually love something other than what they do for a living. To get people thinking, I share what I love.

I love:

- Being a mother
- Performing improv comedy
- The smell of freshly cut grapefruit

If your connection to what you love is clear, you are more fun to talk to and twice as likely to engage those who are listening to you. You're likely to make a greater impact and reach an outcome you hoped to reach with your audience.

Add up the things you love and remember this list. This exercise will help you to remember where you are getting love right and will eliminate the wasted time you're yearning for something you do not have.

WEEK TWO: DAY FOUR

Brief (from by blog, December 15, 2015)

In the past week, two clients told me they would like to develop the skill of "being brief." They feel they talk too much therefore sounding less confident when they communicate.

Mastering and knowing when to activate this skill can mean closing an important deal or simply empowering a colleague or someone we love to something greater.

More than ever, there are forums to share what we know, and the content to communicate and share is endless. Some forums give us a chance to post as much as we like and others require that we say what we need to say in a certain amount of words. Have you ever tried to make your point in 140 characters or less on Twitter? A lesson in brevity!

The most powerful communicators establish and adhere to a pattern with their messages. They design these messages to be extrapolated upon or dispensed in sound bites. They have perfected this skill by knowing who their audience is and what the audience responds to. They also survey or take the temperature of their audience on a regular basis so they're privy to the changing needs of their audience.

Become a great communicator and master brevity with these simple steps:

1. Pause to give.
   Think about saying nothing before you think about saying anything. Before you speak, pause; be your own survey collector and listen for offers in the space. After you pause and receive offers, you know what to give. A perfect improv scene takes off with this technique.

2. Repeat what was said.
   Repeating what someone else has said and affirming and thinking "yes and" helps you to get out of your head and stay with the conversation in that space. Great improvisers practice this during the give and take with characters they have created. Many times we get caught up and say more than we need to because we forget to take what has been given.
3. Follow your favorites
   Limit the feed in your social media outlets to follow your favorite communicators. Let them inspire you to go deep inside yourself and uncover your most powerful words so you can use them the way you were meant to. Enjoy being immersed in the topics you love the most and from the inspiration alone you can uncover crisp messages and learn to deliver them concisely and feeling confident.

My goal for every client is that they increase the number of times they feel effortless when they communicate. When we master being brief, effortlessness ensues.

Week Two: Day Five

Just (from my blog, September 20, 2015)

We all use words that are unnecessary. Working one-on-one with clients, together we carve out certain words they are using that may be keeping them from saying what they want to say or from having their family, friends, or co-workers understand them more clearly.

I call the words they frequently use that may be causing them to be stagnant in their communication, "NO words". We put them in a column and develop an awareness of when we are using them and *practice using them less.*

The words that are light and create a feeling of joy and forward motion are called "YES words." We put those in a column and *practice using them more.*

Just is one of those words we rarely need and overuse.

"Just" is one of the top "NO words" especially for women. I used to use it a lot so I understand the tendency to defer to it.

Good use of the word just:

"We just arrived!"

Bad use of the word just:

I'm just a mom.
I'm just here to help my friend.
I just want to understand what you're saying.
I just can't figure out what to do here.

Take a look at each of the sentences above and say them to yourself out loud and REMOVE the word "just" when you do. In fact, take a beat and be silent instead of using the word.

You'll see you do not need the word "just" in most cases. The statement sounds clearer, more confident and you may even feel more powerful when you say the above sentences—even the "good use" version—without it.

Here is what the above sentences look like without *just*:

Good use of the word just:

I am a mom.
I'm here to help my friend.
I want to understand what you're saying.
I can't figure out what to do here.

Say them out loud to yourself and feel the difference.

Try this practice when you re-enter your life today. Pay attention to the word "Just" and see how often—if at all—you really need it.

Week Two: Day Six

Easier (from my blog, July 22, 2015)

Life is not easy.

I used to work hard to not say that because the focus of my work is on what is easy. This statement worked against my mantra. It's hard for me to write and harder to say because all the words surrounding the word YES are light and make it sound like "easy" is part of the package.

The reality is *life* is hard and my work is to help people uncover something easier, no matter what happens in their lives. Some of us endure countless disappointments and are left feeling like the drama will never end.

Recently, I completed coaching with a client and together we uncovered some interesting patterns in a typical day that were contributing to his heavy feelings. He has a crazy schedule with considerable time spent out of the office—his weekends were getting eaten up with emails and organizing his work.

One strategy we uncovered was so effective and easy to implement. His response was, "Things seem easier now."

The Fix

Strive for one personal interaction at a time. The best spaces to enter are the ones with beating hearts (this means in person) especially if you are looking for feedback or to be distracted from the thoughts or lists that are making you feel heavy.

Call friends more often instead of relying on social media and texting for personal feedback. Regularly *talk to someone* outside the sphere of work. Even if it was to have conversations five minutes here and ten minutes there, do this two to four times a day.

The outcomes of my client's new practice:

- Others were happy to hear from him.
- He found out he was needed only to listen (not work!) to people who valued and loved him.
- He thought of great ideas for networking and even planning a vacation by reaching out in person with his voice.
- Originally he thought the distraction would keep him from getting his work done and he found quite the opposite. The increased human interaction helped to clear up his feeling of dread and sparked his creativity.
- He experienced relief by hearing how others were doing.

With the same job and the same address and the same life he has increased the number of times things have felt easier simply by reaching beyond his space and entering new ones. Spaces are filled with offers and a seasoned improviser knows this well.

There is always an easier new space. There is always time to enter one.

Take it for yourself.

Week Two: Day Seven

Trip (from my blog, May 23, 2015)

Last month, I took a trip with my men, James (sixteen) and Harry (thirteen), to visit a few colleges James is considering when he applies next year. In six days, we covered five campuses in four states. The trip was planned down to the minute as some of the stops were two hours apart and the tours/visits lasted four to six hours.

We worked as a team for the betterment of one of us. We gathered stats on the schools, we explored the campuses and we toured the surrounding area. We sought advisors in the subject areas James wanted to study. We had an obligation to gather as much information as we could on this trip—this was his future, after all!

Although we had a very purposeful goal on this trip, and it required a serious approach, we also enjoyed other experiences along the way, the *present*. A visit with a close college friend was opted for instead of another advisor meeting. Choosing our seats at the welcome/information sessions became a fun game because the front rows were always empty. These were our seats and we knew exactly where to go in these rooms we had never been before.

We included a visit to an important battlefield. After spending two hours at what we were sure was the right one, we drove to our hotel only to pass the entrance to the real battlefield on the way. We laughed and were barely bothered. We loved what we saw of what we were sure was the real deal.

The trip was one to plan for the future and the greatest moments came when we enjoyed the present.

When you plan your trips this summer, remember these special trip tips:

1. The front row is always available.
2. Opportunity for a great connection trumps the plan.
3. Every site taken in together is the right site.

Week Three: Day One

Model (from my blog, March 31, 2015)

I have the "model walk" down solid. You know the one seen on the runway, showing the styles for next year? One hand on my hip, the other dangling like spaghetti, my eyes staring forward, and then a horse-like strut lifting my legs and stomping as I walk.

The model walk comes out when I'm trying to be silly with friends or during an improv warm-up with music. I love to entertain those around me and get a good laugh.

But aside from the fun that comes from doing the model walk, it's freeing. The long and lanky woman intent on moving forward to demonstrate the flow of the frock she is presenting. It uncovers my inner performer, and it feels powerful!

When I enter spaces as a mother, speaker and coach, I'm aware that what I model makes an impact. If I am suggesting my children read, have they seen me with a book in my hand? If I'm advising my clients to manage their time well, did I start our call on time and relay how my schedule makes time for self-care? If I am impressing upon an audience to embrace their joy do I smile when I say that and physically appear joyful when I do?

A great way to teach people to be better communicators is to model it. A great way to teach almost anyone to do almost anything is to model it.

Are you the model you would like to be? Practice these simple steps and see how it feels.

3 Steps to Being a Good Model

1. Talk the talk and walk the walk. Be what you say you are and do so with conviction.
2. Listen to your audience: Make sure you know who you are talking to. The most powerful way to do that is to get them talking!
3. Wear it. Believe in what you are modeling and be doubt free and people will see what you are modeling from the energy you generate before you even speak.

WEEK THREE: DAY TWO

Voice (from my blog, November 7, 2014)

You were born with a voice. Your voice gives you the power to communicate what you want in every space you enter. You transfer that power to a gadget when you type or text what you want to say. Don't get me wrong, I love these gadgets because they enable me to be many things to many people and they give me the chance to convey lots of messages at the same time at record speed.

The use of these gadgets makes me feel empowered in the short run. In the long run they make me feel disconnected.

When we develop a habit of typing in order to communicate any number of messages (instead of speaking) we may experience a few unwanted side effects. We may develop a fear of saying what we really want to say. We may develop a fear of getting into conflict of any kind. We may make-up what we think people are thinking instead asking them to tell us what they are thinking. We may do this over and over again and create miscommunication and waste a lot of precious time.

Here are some suggestions for checking in with yourself when you're using a gadget.

1. Dial a number and have a real conversation when you think you have gotten too far into an email or text exchange and it begins to lack clarity.
2. Notice how you feel when you use your voice. The inflections you hear will help to reassure you in the conversation. When you hear the voice of the other person you may experience relief.
3. Catch yourself the next time you look at a gadget for feedback and look forward and up. There is likely someone or something right in front of you that you may not have seen if you were typing.

That's it! Awareness is the solution. These three simple steps will give you comfort when you start using them today.

Your voice is your most powerful tool. Use it!

Week Three: Day Three

Parents (from my blog, September 12, 2014)

This is a big month for most parents. It is the beginning of a new school year for the children we manage on a daily basis and many words apply: binders, tryouts, loose-leaf, lunch money, schedule, test, homework, snack, bus stop, pencils.

Those words, along with the sound of crickets, are a reminder of how nice it can be to return to another year and a chance for our children to start again with new classrooms and new teachers.

It is also an opportunity to think about what we can do better as parents and solve problems before they affect our children. We can buy all the supplies on the list, we can pack the perfect lunch, we can be on time to pick them up at practice and we can hire a tutor to help them prepare for an upcoming test. We can sit and listen to the stories about their day and respect them when they wish to sit silently and say nothing. We can hug them and tell them we love them and be there when they need us.

We cannot always make everything perfect or prevent the times they will feel defeated and stressed.

What we *can* do is model *what* to do when things don't happen as planned. Share the experiences we have with our "teachers" and how we learn from them. We can talk about our lunch meeting and why we thought it went well. We can talk about the countless "tests" we get through and how we felt we scored or how we recovered when we failed.

As parents we enter "classrooms" all the time and the experience we have in these spaces is worth sharing now. Our children are ready to learn from us. Communicate to them and help build them strong by teaching how we manage in our own daily classrooms.

Week Three: Day Four

Snapshot (from my blog, August 12, 2014)

Two weeks ago I put my children on a plane to spend the weekend with my brother and sister-in-law in Minneapolis.

Their early flight meant we had to be at the airport by 5:00 a.m. I also had a very important meeting that was months in the planning that started at 9:00 a.m. Their flight would take off at 7:15 a.m. and of course I wanted to be there to watch them board.

This preponderance of details was taking over my thinking and keeping me from being present with them until while on the escalator, I glanced down at their handsome faces and turned to take a picture.

From that point on I snapped away. As they headed to the gate, I took a picture. As they ate their breakfast I took a picture. As they sat and fiddled with their gadgets, I took a picture. After they hugged me and said goodbye and walked past the agents to board the plane…I took one last picture.

My men are a big part of my life right now and the two decades they will spend in this space with me will be over some day. Then they will be part of my life in a different way.

This was a snapshot in my life and theirs and I woke up just in time to be present in it and trust that everything that needed to happen later would happen as planned.

They boarded the plane on time and I made it home to shower, get the train and arrive at my meeting with ten whole minutes to spare. Because I allowed myself to be affected by the time with my men, I can tell you, I was really relaxed all day. It occurred to me this whole day unfolded the way it should have because of me, and the awareness that continually shapes my life. The principles whose foundations steer my communications and actions are: Enter Free, Say YES, Give and Receive and Transform. It's a very powerful tool when you have the awareness to be in a space, stay in the space and receive in the space. The space becomes yours.

Summers present many opportunities to get out of our heads, be present, take in what is right in front of us. Most of these moments seem small, but when added together, the picture is very big.

Take a snapshot and enjoy!

Week Three: Day Five

Connections (from my blog, July 15, 2013)

I just returned from the Omega Institute where I attended a workshop with Brian Weiss called Miracles Happen, based on his book by the same name. Doctor Weiss is a leader on past life regression therapy.

The workshop was recommended to me by a friend who had been to one of my talks and thought it would interest me. On the website I was struck by the description about strengthening your intuition. This past year I have been connected to my intuition more than ever before and I wanted to be more connected to it. The past life piece just sounded cool. So I registered.

My first connection was to Doctor Weiss. He is *very funny!* His soothing voice and wry sense of humor made it a pleasure to listen to him. As a group we were guided to deep meditation. This guided state was similar to that period before you wake from sleep and you are "almost" aware of your surroundings.

Over the weekend we were guided into regressions, progressions and psychometry.

The latter is an exercise in which you hand an object to a partner, preferably a stranger. They may discover facts about an event or person based on the inanimate object.

My second connection was to Mickey. We had met the night before after registering. While walking we introduced ourselves and moved on. The next morning, in a room of over 300 people, she was siting behind me and became my partner for this exercise. I gave her a relic that had been given to me by my grandmother in 1997.

Doctor Weiss had us all be silent with the piece and hold it close to us and then share what came to mind with our partner. I had Mickey's watch and saw the same image of her over and over again. I saw her face framed in blue and felt Joy while looking at her. When I repeated it to her she said she had come to Omega seeking joy, simple joy. I felt better because I really wanted to find more but she was quite pleased and gave me a big smile when I reported my "Vision."

Then she told me mine. She saw a man who looked like me smiling at me and she saw a hammer. She saw a woman with the man who was constantly smiling and laughing and happy. The woman was on a porch and there was lemonade and the man was in a golf cart on a path. He was sitting in the cart saying he was proud of me and his cart was on a long path. She said, "He is *like* you." She described my grandparents and the scenes from a video I made of them the weekend my grandmother gave me the relic Mickey was holding.

When I showed her the picture of my grandparents, she started crying and said that was the woman she saw. The man was a younger version of my grandfather but the same face. I am still trying to figure out the presence of the hammer but the other pieces of her vision were spot on. My connection to my grandparents was very strong when they were alive and I think of them every day. Mickey connected to this vivid memory from an object that connected me to them.

Phew!

In the span of three days I did not have a past life regression. I did see many images but never walked through a scene from the past. Doctor Weiss told us that kind of experience takes practice. The clear connection to my grandparents and other events and images uncovered while I was in a peaceful state was rich, really rich.

While I was on line for registration, lunch, dinner, and enjoying a walk in the labyrinth on campus I made other beautiful connections. It was a pleasure to meet: Liz the Yogi, Lorraine the Horse Whisperer, Karen the Healer, Denise the Anesthesiologist, Dana, the Bag Blogger and of course, Mickey, who saw my grandparents.

Omega is a space for healing. You don't need to be broken to be there. In fact, the balance of people seeking deep healing and those coming for an affirmation or strengthening (me) created a beautiful circle of energy and ultimately powerful connections.

People were there to receive and share and connect.

In this crazy world, personal connections are harder and harder to make because we can often carry our heavy loads into the spaces we enter. I was there to learn more about my intuition and what I learned was that we never know when we are going to make a connection. Allowing space for stillness makes us more of aware of these connections and what they mean over the long term.

Doctor Weiss explained on the first night that when we made contact with this part of our souls we are identifying unconditional love. It is our basic human desire to be connected to others and to have relationships that fill our hearts.

This was empowering, cool stuff. Facing a new week is a lot easier after having a weekend like this!

Week Three: Day Six

Banter (from my blog, March 1, 2013)

I learned the power of banter from my grandfather. He was the Chairman of Toastmasters of Long Island, a top salesperson for Liberty Mutual, a volunteer in his community, a fun guy to play golf with and a man with the gift of gab. He was one of the most powerful influences in my life.

The kind of banter I enjoyed with him on a regular basis is harder to find these days. I was lucky enough to enjoy it last night with a former colleague who has become an invaluable friend and this morning with my little men. These moments gave me food for thought and filled my heart.

The conveniences we enjoy with advances in technology are infinite. Yet, it has in some cases removed the fulfilling elements of live exchange from our day.

See what you can do this weekend to turn off the gadgets and look into more faces, listen to and tell some stories. If there were cameras in heaven, I would be able to show you a pro at work. Here's to my Pa and the power of banter.

WEEK THREE: DAY SEVEN

Mother (from my blog, May 9, 2014)

This word conjures up all kinds of thoughts and emotions.

Many of us feel love, warmth and comfort, while others feel conflict, duty and guilt.

I have felt all of these from the moment I became a mother.

Over time, "Mother" has transcended tradition. In some homes, there are two moms, and in others there is a dad or a grandmother who are taking over the role of mother. Aunts and close friends without children show up in children's lives in a nurturing way when needed. There are "host moms" to student exchange students who must fill both a cultural and emotional gap for up to a year.

Mothers show up in many ways and no matter what part of the world you live in, the language is the same. A few weeks ago, I was in the stands watching my son's water polo match. There was a woman seated in front of me who I could tell was rooting for our team but I had never seen her before. She pointed to the exchange student and I understood by her signals that she didn't speak English, and this was her son. She was visiting on a brief holiday from Spain.

As we watched the games together, we pointed and laughed and shrieked and cheered and shed some tears. When it was over, we hugged and she pointed to her camera and indicated that she would share photos she took of my son. I gave her my card. We nodded, smiled and shared our only mutually understood word, "Yes." We shared so many more unspoken words, as mothers.

Embrace your thoughts and emotions and be still with the role you have with "Mother"—we learn more from this relationship than any other in our lives.

Week Four: Day One

Course (from my blog, April 25, 2014)

Recently, a coaching client of mine enjoyed valuable closure after a stressful few months with a colleague. It was such a powerful outcome I wanted to share how he got there because often people feel like they are in a negative environment indefinitely.

In life, we are confronted with people who are *not* the yin to our yang and we have to exist in spaces with these people either as co-workers or family members and sometimes both. The stress can become unbearable: distracting and divisive, not to mention the toll it takes on our health.

How do you resolve this in a way that is truly satisfying?

Be true to who you are. Stay the course. Think for yourself and do not think for the other person. We can only control how we respond to people, what we bring to the space. If you speak or behave outside of who you are, the conflict mounts and the aggressor wins.

Choose your words and stay the course. Release yourself from trying to control what happens next.

My client stayed the course. He confronted his aggressor yet remained patient and positive about his work. The difficult colleague suddenly became difficult for others, and eventually moved on. Now my client notices more of the personalities he loves to work with coming into his life. By staying the course you *will* get to the other side of conflict, and back to happiness and productivity.

Week Four: Day Two

Feedback (from my blog, April 3, 2014)

Are you getting the feedback you crave?

I'm not talking about "Likes" or "New Connections" in social media. I'm talking about hearing what you need to hear in order to know if your message is having a positive impact on your audience.

A coaching client recently said to me, "People think I'm intense." I asked if someone had actually said that to her and she said, "No, but in the absence of feedback I'm making that assumption."

I wondered how many assumptions we all make in a day in the absence of feedback.

Ed Koch, former mayor of New York, was well known for saying, "How'm I doing?" He met people on their level and with this simple question was able to engage any audience at any time. People love to tell you what they think and are flattered you thought enough about them to ask their opinion.

Gathering feedback helps us figure out if we are on the right path to our goals and success.

What is the best way to get feedback? I have three simple steps:

1. Identify your safe messengers. Safe messengers are people whose opinion you trust and respect.
2. Ask about a specific topic, telling them why you need the feedback and the goals you have for the results.
3. Once you implement their feedback, be sure to measure results and give your messenger this feedback—it will keep them invested and engaged in your goals and provide a constant resource for new feedback.

Are you getting regular feedback from people you trust in both your professional and personal life? I train my audiences to communicate effectively so both sides are getting the valuable feedback they need, leaving them empowered to move toward their desired outcomes.

Try these 3 simple steps and please give me *your* feedback!

Week Four: Day Three

Transform (from my blog, February 27, 2014)

On this last storm effort, my only shovel broke and I was out of salt. More snow and ice were expected overnight so I set out to Home Depot for supplies. As I walked into the store, I was surprised not to see the prominent shovel display at the front door. I looked up for a sign to tell me which aisle to find "winter tools" and there was nothing. After searching for someone to direct me, I finally got my answer: we are out of shovels and salt.

Defeated, I got in my car and drove home.

Tense and returning without what I needed, I pulled out the broken shovel and began to do what I could. Tears welled in my eyes because I was tired and it was dark and icy and I was quite simply, spent.

Then I heard someone say, "You shouldn't be doing that." I looked up and a friend of a friend, John, re-introduced himself and took the shovel from me. With great speed, he started to clear the driveway. I ran and got the ice pick so I could contribute to the process.

We were chatting about the crazy weather when he said, "We went to your improv show in December." I said, "Oh my gosh, thank you for reminding me! What was your favorite part or scene?"

He replied, "Actually I can't remember one in particular, I just remember how great it felt to laugh that hard."

It was so nice to get that feedback and in that moment, I forgot about all the inconveniences I had been through. We chatted more and in no time, he had finished the job. The snow was cleared and I had a smile on my face.

The inconvenience and stress were transformed by a wonderful helper and his words. The improvisation moment of transforming by saying YES came to life so organically when I accepted help: "a character is different at the end of an improv scene based on the events that changed them, bringing new perspectives and reactions."

Let it snow!

Week Four: Day Four

What Gloria Steinem Taught Me About Faith (appeared in *Huffington Post*, December 6, 2017)

Recently I had the chance to hear Gloria Steinem speak in a small setting about her life, her recent work and the state of the women's movement to date.

She read from her most recent book, *My Life on the Road* and answered questions of the moderator and members of the audience with refreshing presence.

She is quite simply, ethereal and peaceful in person. The depths of Gloria Steinem's understanding of what it has meant to be a woman during the eighty-two years she has been on this planet were conveyed with every word she uttered.

I felt calm and connected to her even sitting in the audience. I was eager to know what I could learn from her that I hadn't already read in one of her books or seen in an interview she had given.

It was apparent in the ease with which she answered questions that she was doing so from the clearest possible place in her heart. A long time ago, Gloria Steinem figured out what she was here to do and she's been doing it.

When she was asked what some of the initial motivation to put herself out there was, she said, "The women's movement came along and I discovered I was happy."

When she was asked about the inspiration of Bring Your Daughter to Work Day, which she launched in conjunction with The Ms. Foundation she said,

"If you can't see it, you can't be it."

When she was asked about education and women she said:

"Women's colleges produce more women who do non-traditional things."

On the topic of men and finding a great partner she said,

"Find one who makes you feel smart, wants you to achieve all your dreams and makes you laugh."

On bringing change to the world she said,

"Be a witness. Take action. Lead to activism. Organize across boundaries. Improve the standards of success."

The last question was "What advice would you give to your younger self?" Gloria said,

"Everything's going to be all right."

And there, at that moment, I was set free. My strong faith was now even stronger. God had been making this point to me in prayer my entire life and here was Gloria Steinem live with one sentence helping me to expand my faith in the world and perhaps most importantly to expand my faith in me.

I felt lighter and like someone had just exposed me to the Holy Grail of thoughts for the future and how to live in the now.

I too, could choose to be her younger self and I could take what she was telling me or ignore it because I had so much to worry about that she didn't know about.

Imagine where our hearts and minds could take us if our mission was as clear to each of us as Gloria Steinem's mission is to her? Imagine where our hearts and minds could take us if we had enough faith to know that the things we may be worrying about may in fact be a distraction from what we are here to do.

"Everything's going to be all right."

We don't know what is going to happen in our lives but if we can go forward believing and having faith that everything will be all right then we are sure to see what we are here to do and do it, like Gloria.

Week Four: Day Five

Fired on Friday the 13th and Three Ways to Move Forward (from my blog in the *Huffington Post*, November 13, 2015)

On Friday, November 13, 1992 I was fired from my job as a fundraiser at a non-profit I loved on the day I was to receive my one-year review.

I was devastated because my track record in this one and all the jobs I held up to that point had been successful, very successful. I was devastated because the grounds for my firing were not there; an internal personality conflict—I had been warned about—was the real reason I was walked out of the building that morning after the very brief annual-review-turned-firing. I was devastated because I had left the world of political fundraising so I could use my prowess for asking for money for a good cause and improve the lives of others.

I couldn't imagine a personality conflict would cost me my job when the goal of the work we were doing was to improve the quality of life for people with disease.

I wanted desperately to have my case heard and to correct the misinformation about me. If the right people heard me, my name could be cleared.

When I proposed reaching out to the chair of the non-profit and to the board members who knew me, my father, a lawyer and my great advisor said, "write the letter you would like to write, read it, throw it away and move on."

I took his advice and did that. Twelve weeks later I had a new job raising money for a campaign for mayor in an office eight blocks from the non-profit offices. In our meeting the candidate said he wanted to "improve the quality of life for New Yorkers."

A little over a year later, sitting in my new City Hall office as a result of my candidate's win, I received a hand written letter from the person who was instrumental in having me fired (the source of the personality conflict). She congratulated me on my new post after she had read about it in the paper. After the congratulations, she asked if I would help her secure my new boss, Mayor Giuliani for an event to help the non-profit from which I had been fired.

Later, during a scheduling meeting I was asked if his participation in an event for this cause would be a good use of Rudy's time and I said, yes.

I kept the beautifully written note of congratulations and request for help in my desk that day and in the many desks I operated from for years. I kept it as a reminder that life moves on and we need to move on with it. She moved on. I moved on. I gained nothing by lamenting over all that was wrong with my firing and gained plenty by ridding myself of the anger and disappointment.

As a result, I found a place to use my talents and give back in a different position than the one I originally envisioned.

The key lessons learned from this Friday the Thirteenth firing came over time and became clearer the further away I got from that bad day.

1. Be Sad.
   Yup. Take it in. Feel everything that comes with the loss of something you counted on that ended in a way you had no control over. It's awful. Take the time to be sad.

2. Get Your Power Back.
   Check. You've been sad. Now it's time to get moving. While the wounds may not have healed, moving forward is the best way to uncover why it happened. It's also important to remember that whoever "did" it to you has moved on. If you keep the sadness and anger in your heart, you give away your power.

3. Be open.
   Your chance to use your talents to improve lives may be in a different place than the one you envisioned. Be open to the offers in the new spaces you may enter after your firing.

Week Four: Day Six

6 Steps to Get Unstuck Thinking YES! (from my blog post for Medium on March 15, 2017)

If you are stuck in some area of your life now, these steps are designed to help you become unstuck.

You may be stuck now because of a situation in the past where you achieved a bad result after initiating a project or simple communication with colleagues, friends or family members. The memory of this experience may cause you to feel skittish about moving to take that step again.

We've all been there and the way forward is simple.

Knowing how and when to use YES in our communication enables you to regularly take risks and grow despite what you remember about the past.

The following six steps will activate your YES and keep the relationship building force inside of you alive.

1. Stay in Touch
   Absence makes the heart grow doubt. When we have not heard from someone we tend think of bad things that are imaginary, not true. If you've been out of touch with someone and wonder why, pick up the phone. Check in. Take down the barriers you've built from wondering what was wrong.

2. Think for Yourself
   Do not think for other people. When we spend time imagining what other people are thinking we use a lot of energy that could otherwise be used to create for someone who needs us. This is similar to the first step because it's that much of a factor in our state of stuck.

3. Receive

   There are plenty of offers to receive in every space you enter. You will see them when you're ready to receive them. Practice openness and stillness and you will see what you are here to see so you can do what you are here to do.

4. Love Your Time

   You have the time. Shape your time by referring to it as what you have rather than what you do not have. Use your time to do, rather than to say what you cannot do.

5. Note The Space Between

   There are two kinds of spaces; the one you occupy when there is activity and the one in-between the activity. The space between is an opportunity to restore and refresh and get ready for the next activity. Be mindful of both.

6. Be Passionate

   Let loose. Make sure you are your true self in every space you enter. Feed what you are passionate about and be in spaces with people who share your passion.

Be mindful of the steps above and you will always be able to become unstuck while thinking YES.

Week Four: Day Seven

This is the blog I wrote for the *Huffington Post* to commemorate my fiftieth birthday in 2016. The response to the personal things I shared inspired me to continue to share this way and to write this book. On this last day of launching the power of YES in YOU, consider writing a list of what you want to take with you. Look back on what you've written over the past four weeks and take what moves you and makes you smile. Do it. Share it. Give it to yourself everyday!

50 Things I'm Taking With Me to My Next 50 Years

The past 50 years have included a whole lot. I have had more jobs than I can count. I've been fired. I've been married. I've been divorced. I've given birth. I've fought for my children. I've lived in fancy places. I've lived in simple places. I've been 50 pounds heavier. I've slept in a tent. I've slept in five-star hotels. I've run birthday parties for preschoolers and election parties for presidents. I've raised money and I've raised awareness.

My 50th birthday celebration feels like a rite of passage and does not scare or depress me at all. It feels good. To be honest, I have never felt better physically and more in tune with myself mentally and spiritually.

I still feel pain, I get mad, I suffer setbacks and think of tweaking this or that when I look in the mirror but overall I've become my own cheerleader and because of that more positive things seem to be happening around me.

We are the sum of the experiences in our lives. There comes a point when we know what we need to take with us to get where we're going. As I enter the next 50 years these are 50 things I'll take with me:

1. I'll take my best investment, me.
2. I'll take *every* ounce of moisturizer I can get my hands on.
3. I'll take looking into people's eyes more.

4. I'll take a walk on the beach as often as I can make it happen.
5. I'll take feeling over not feeling.
6. I'll take warmth and connection.
7. I'll take Champagne *and* Gin.
8. I'll take praying for someone who's causing me pain over letting it eat away at me.
9. I'll take breathing.
10. I'll take saying "I love you" more.
11. I'll take laughing.
12. I'll take the *joy* of being the mother of my princes, James and Harry.
13. I'll take more time to be present for my princes, James and Harry.
14. I'll take sharing the memories of this past 50 and fully living in next 50 with incredible friends.
15. I'll take hugs and focus on being the last one to let go.
16. I'll take humility.
17. I'll take my newfound money saving technique of using half a dryer sheet instead of the whole one because those things are expensive!
18. I'll take cashmere anything.
19. I'll take Humor.
20. I'll take Grace.
21. I'll take Spirit.
22. I'll take diplomacy.

23. I'll take my scale because it's helped me stay true to my commitment to myself.
24. I'll take the moon and take more time to take it in.
25. I'll take the sun as long as I'm wearing a nice big hat!
26. I'll take the people I love and be ready for new love.
27. I'll take the events I plan.
28. I'll take the events I don't plan.
29. I'll take suggestions from a trusted few.
30. I'll take my rosary beads.
31. I'll take my college roommates.
32. I'll take essential oils.
33. I'll take my freckles (the exact number I have and no more).
34. I'll take yoga.
35. I'll take my books on Jackie Kennedy, Ronald Reagan and Shirley MacLaine.
36. I'll take *Terms of Endearment*, my favorite movie.
37. I'll take *A Fish Called Wanda*, my favorite comedy.
38. I'll take *Ave Maria*, my favorite song.
39. I'll take (only fresh) candy corn.
40. I'll take my inner Goddess.
41. I'll take smiling over not smiling.
42. I'll take all the elephants I have collected and visions of the ones I will ride.
43. I'll take the letters and cards from my children.
44. I'll take chocolate.
45. I'll take what I need from "NO."

46. I'll take *thank you* and never abbreviate it.
47. I'll take every stage I can as an improviser, speaker and messenger for positivity.
48. I'll take more time to play golf.
49. I'll take waking up.
50. I'll take—*and give*—"YES" all day, everyday.

ABOUT THE AUTHOR

Jeanne M. Stafford is a professional speaker, comedy improviser, political junkie, and mother of two teenaged boys and Lambeau, their yellow lab. Jeanne's mission is to communicate the Power of YES to every individual she meets through her speaking and training. Her audiences learn how communicating like a comedy improviser shrinks our time in conflict and increases our productivity at work and home.

Jeanne's clients and audiences asked, "How do you do it? How are you happy? What do you do to keep your energy up?" and in response she wrote this interactive handbook-style book.

Jeanne is a member of The National Speakers Association and is the host of Jeanne Stafford's Networking Dinner in New York City where she hosts fellow speakers and creates a space for leaders to grow in their communication.

In her free time, Jeanne enjoys being with her children, volunteering on several nonprofit boards, wearing Chanel No. 5, drinking gin, and playing golf.

Visit Jeanne and receive 30 Days of YES at:
jeannemstafford.com
Twitter: @JeanneStafford
Instagram: jeanne_stafford
Facebook: Jeanne M. Stafford